My Ántonia

My Ántonia

a play

FROM THE NOVEL BY
Willa Cather

ADAPTED FOR THE STAGE BY
Jarrett Dapier

AGATITE PRESS
EVANSTON, ILLINOIS
2013

Agatite Press
ISBN-13: 978-0-61581-980-8
ISBN-10: 0-61581-980-X

Design and composition by Barbara Evans

SPECIAL THANKS

Gary Ambler and the Celebration Company at the Station Theatre for being game.

Joi Hoffsommer for her editing acumen.

Barbara Evans for her book design and composition.

Christopher Shinn for his guidance and support.

PRODUCTION HISTORY

The world première of *My Ántonia* was produced by the Celebration Company at the Station Theatre (Rick Orr, Artistic Director) in Urbana, Illinois, on December 1, 2011. It was directed by Gary Ambler and Joi Hoffsommer; the producer was Shawna Smith; set design was by Rachel Witt-Callahan; costume design was by Jodi L. Prosser; lighting design was by Darren McCroom; sound design was by Robert Dagit; props were by Jacob Foster; choreographer was S. Alicia Cross Engelhardt; Czech translation and language coach was Alena Bartosova; and the production stage manager was David Swinford.

Narrator Jim	Gary Ambler
Jim Burden	Jesse Angelo
Josiah "Grandpa" Burden	Jeff McGill
Emmaline "Grandma" Burden	Tiffany Joy
Ántonia Shimerda	Stephanie Swearingen
Ambrosch Shimerda	Max Keagle
Mr. Shimerda	Alex Zelck
Mrs. Shimerda	Claire Cowley
Lena Lingard	Karen Hughes
Mrs. Harling	Jodi L. Prosser
Otto Fuchs	Michael Murphy

Frontispiece (*opposite*): "The snow changes the whole world!" Jim (Jesse Angelo) and Ántonia (Stephanie Swearingen) at the Station Theatre in Urbana, Illinois. Photo by Jesse Folks.

NOTES ON CASTING

My Ántonia is meant to be performed by an ensemble of 11–14 actors, with doubling up where possible. NARRATOR JIM, JIM BURDEN, and ÁNTONIA do not double up.

The original production had a cast of 11 performers (5W, 6M) with character assignments as follows.

Narrator Jim—40s

Jim Burden—10–20 years old; 40 years old in final scene

Ántonia Shimerda—14–24; mid-40s in final scene

Mr. Shimerda—late 30s; also plays Larry Donovan/Gaston Cleric

Mrs. Shimerda—late 20s; also plays Lena Lingard and one of Ántonia's children

Ambrosch Shimerda—17; also plays Charley Harling, Harry Payne, and one of Ántonia's children

Grandmother Burden—45–55; also plays Mrs. Harling

Grandfather Burden—45–55; also plays Mr. Harling

Otto Fuchs—late 30s–early 40s; also plays Wick Cutter and one of Ántonia's children

Tiny Soderball—16–20; also plays Sally Harling and one of Ántonia's children

Because it worked well, directors should use these original cast assignments as a recommended guide, but should not feel bound to repeat them exactly. Directors may choose not to double some roles—or choose different double assignments—depending on their situation. One performer who is well suited to play Lena Lingard, for example, may not be right to play Mrs. Shimerda.

Characters

NARRATOR JIM, 40s. Returning to his childhood town for the first time in over 20 years.

JIM BURDEN, a 10-year-old boy at start, transplanted to Nebraska from Virginia after the death of his parents.

EMMALINE "GRANDMOTHER" BURDEN, 50s. Hard-working, quietly nurturing.

JOSIAH "GRANDFATHER" BURDEN, 50s. Hard-working, devout, kind.

ÁNTONIA SHIMERDA, 14 at start. A girl recently emigrated from Bohemia outside Prague to Nebraska.

AMBROSCH SHIMERDA, 17. Her brother.

MR. SHIMERDA, late 30s. Her father.

MRS. SHIMERDA, 30s. Her mother.

OTTO FUCHS, 30–40s. A tireless farmhand who has worked all over the west and Texas.

MRS. HARLING, late 30s. Jim's neighbor in town. Wealthy by local standards.

MR. HARLING, late 30s. Her husband. A wealthy banker.

CHARLEY HARLING, 17. Their son.

SALLY HARLING, 10. Their daughter.

JULIA HARLING, 14. Their daughter. Only heard offstage.

LENA LINGARD, 16 at start. Immigrant girl newly arrived in town from family farm. Norwegian. Sensuous.

TINY SODERBALL, 16 at start. Immigrant girl newly arrived in town from family farm. Also Norwegian.

LARRY DONOVAN, 18–20. A young man in town.

HARRY PAINE, 18–20. A young man in town. Works in banking. Recently engaged to employer's daughter.

GASTON CLERIC, early 30s. Virgil scholar at University of Nebraska. Restless, bright spirit.

WICK CUTTER, 40s. Town creditor. Pitiless.

SETTING

Nebraska, 1880–1920

STAGING

Productions should use an active ensemble and simple theatrical conventions to convey the expansiveness of the prairie, the seasons, work, and hardship. Use all corners of the space, all levels, so that the changing prairie is all around us. By seeing the ensemble work during scene changes, the production can convey active physical labor.

WOMEN AND WORK

Production staging should emphasize the work of the women. The women are the beating heart of this story. Their work is grueling, physically demanding, and never at an end.

My Ántonia

ACT I
CHILDHOOD

SCENE 1: TWO ARRIVALS

(The blast of a train whistle, blackout. In the black, we hear the deafening sound of a train approaching, stopping and idling. A lantern appears in the black, held by OTTO FUCHS. He's a desperado-looking man who might have stepped out of the pages of a Jesse James book: lively, quick, powerful, and light on his feet. There is activity going on in the dark, movement of figures removing trunks and baggage from the train. The conductor yells out "BLACK HAWK! BLACK HAWK!" The sound of four people speaking fast Czech simultaneously is heard all around us. The effect of the noise, the movement in the dark and the dim lantern-light casting swinging shadows should be disorienting. We begin to sense the presence of a family of four who have entered from the back of the house and are walking up the aisle with uncertainty. On the other side of the house a boy of 10, equally intimidated, moves toward the stage. Conductor shouts: "LAST CALL BLACK HAWK!" OTTO must shout over the noise and swing his lantern to cut light through the steam.)

OTTO: Burden! Looking for Jim Burden!

JIM: Here!

OTTO: Jimmy?

JIM: Yep!

OTTO: I'm Otto Fuchs. I work for your grandfather.

JIM: Hello!

ÁNTONIA (*to OTTO*): Hello? Hello? Please. We go Black-Hawk-Nebraska.

> *Scene freezes.*
> *NARRATOR JIM enters with a bag.*

NARRATOR JIM: I was ten years old. I had just lost both my mother and father and was being sent from Virginia to live with my grandparents in Nebraska.

God, this land!

Never-ending miles of ripe wheat, bright-flowered pastures and oak groves wilting in the sun, the dust, the heat, the burning wind, the color and smell of strong weeds and heavy harvests . . . my mind plunges away from me into my childhood, my own infinitesimal past. Memories fill my head and heart completely, as water soaks cloth.

And always I think of one central figure, a Bohemian girl I once knew when I was a boy in Black Hawk. To hear her name is to start a quiet drama in my brain. She means to me the country, the conditions, the whole adventure of my childhood.

It was here I first saw her. That first deep black Nebraska night of my youth, when her family and I arrived after what seemed an interminable train ride across the great midland plain of North America, was as unreal and endless as a dream.

I seem to always begin there. In dreams. In darkness.

But, first, her name.

Pause.

Ántonia.

Train whistle. Scene resumes. Sounds of train preparing to leave.

ÁNTONIA (*to OTTO*): Hello? Hello? Please. We go Black-Hawk-Nebraska.

OTTO: You Krajiek's folks? Krajiek? (*She nods.*) He's looking for you down by the first carriage. (*He points and urges her along. He calls out to Krajiek.*) HEY! Over here!

HEY! Hier drüben!

ÁNTONIA: Much thank! (*"Mama, Papa! Over here!"*): Maminko, Tatínku! Tady jsem!

CONDUCTOR (*off*): ALL CLEAR!!!

ÁNTONIA (*"Where are the trunks?! Tell Ambrosch to bring them this way!"*): Kde jsou truhly? Ať je Ambrož přinese!

MRS. SHIMERDA (*"Are you sure that's him? He's not helping us."*): Je to on? Nepomáhá nám.

ÁNTONIA (*"I don't know!"*): Nevím!

They move past JIM and OTTO toward Krajiek. JIM watches after them, transfixed by their language.

OTTO: Tell me, Jimmy, ain't you scared to come so far west?

JIM: No!

OTTO (*laughing, hoisting JIM's trunk*): Alright then. Well, let's get on the hike. We got a long night's ride ahead of us. We'll follow the other newcomers.

They climb aboard a carriage. NARRATOR JIM joins them, sitting next to JIM. The train leaves the station with a rush of steam.

OTTO: Here we go!

They ride in the darkness. The sky above them is full of stars.

NARRATOR JIM: There seemed to be nothing to see. There was nothing but land: not a country at all, but the material out of which countries are made.

OTTO: You're going to like the farm.

JIM peers out at the darkness, at the stars.

OTTO: Try to sleep.

NARRATOR JIM: But, I couldn't. I had left my parents' spirits behind me. Between that earth and that sky I felt erased, blotted out.

I did not say my prayers that night: here, I felt, what would be, would be.

Blackout.

SCENE 2: YOU LOOK JUST LIKE HIM

(Bright morning light. GRANDMOTHER sits looking at JIM asleep. She is crying. JIM wakes up, sees her. She does not notice. She composes herself, notices that JIM is awake. She smiles.)

GRANDMOTHER (*tender*): Hello.

Pause.

GRANDMOTHER: Had a good sleep?

Pause.
JIM nods slightly.

GRANDMOTHER: Do you know who I am?

Pause.

GRANDMOTHER: There are clean clothes for you on the chair.

JIM: Grandmother.

GRANDMOTHER (*calling out*): Josiah! He's up!

Pause.

GRANDMOTHER: My, how you do look like your father.

GRANDFATHER enters, stands.

GRANDFATHER: There he is.

JIM stands. GRANDFATHER walks to him, holds him by the shoulders, hugs him. Kisses his forehead. Speaks to him softly, kindly.

GRANDFATHER: Good trip?

JIM: Yes, fine. Yes.

GRANDFATHER: Long way to come.

JIM: Yes.

GRANDFATHER: Longer than I ever traveled at your age.

GRANDMOTHER: A right brave little boy, I'd say.

> *JIM smiles.*

GRANDFATHER: Yes. See Chicago?

JIM (*nods*): I saw a family, too. On the train.

GRANDMOTHER: New neighbors, I think. They have a girl a little older.

JIM: I saw her. She spoke . . . words.

GRANDFATHER: Bohemian, I believe.

GRANDMOTHER: We'll be bringing them some provisions this morning.

GRANDFATHER: Soon as Otto's finished with morning work.

> *Pause.*

GRANDMOTHER: You're home.

JIM: Yes.

> *GRANDPARENTS exit. JIM gets dressed, peers through the window excitedly, runs out of the room.*

Scene 3: The Prairie and the Bohemians

(The prairie appears around JIM, created swiftly across the stage by OTTO and others in the ensemble. The bare stage should be transformed simply and it should contain movement and we should see the actors work. Repetitive, ongoing, strenuous. The sound design riffs on the sounds of scythes at work, the sounds of wind in the grass. OTTO begins working to create the carriage. JIM explores as this takes place.)

NARRATOR JIM: The land was bigger than anything I had ever seen. Everywhere as far as the eye could reach, there was nothing but rough, shaggy, red grass. I wanted to walk straight on through it and over the edge of the world.

> *The land moves.*

OTTO (*calling*): Careful a' rattlesnakes, Jim! Knock him on the head you meet one!

> *Throws him a rattlesnake cane. JIM catches it, stands absorbed by the sights.*

GRANDMOTHER: We're off now, Jim! Come along!

> *JIM runs through the fields, back to the carriage, hops on. They ride through the grass.*

GRANDMOTHER: I hate to think of them spending the winter in that cave of Krajiek's . . . it's no better than a badger hole.

OTTO: Probably colder.

GRANDMOTHER: And he's made them pay ten times what it's worth, according to Ole Iverson.

OTTO: Yes'm, and sold 'em his two old bony horses for the price of good workteams. Those horses ain't worth nothing!

GRANDMOTHER: No garden, no hen house . . .

OTTO: He's the only one can talk to them in their language, too. He can tell them anything. And does! If it serves him—

GRANDMOTHER: Who would do such a thing?

> *The carriage stops. A dugout is revealed. MRS. SHIMERDA and ÁNTONIA emerge from within.*

MRS. SHIMERDA: Ah! Very glad! Very glad!

> *Runs to GRANDMOTHER, clamps her hands in her own, wrings them.*

MRS. SHIMERDA (*"The house is no good!!! Krajiek sold us a shit box!"*): Dúm není dobrý. Krajiek nám prodal díru na sraní!

> *MRS. SHIMERDA pulls GRANDMOTHER over to view the dugout.*

GRANDMOTHER: Oh . . . goodness—

MRS. SHIMERDA (*"It's a hellhole!"*): Je to díra do pekel!

> *MRS. SHIMERDA spits on the ground.*

GRANDMOTHER: A *little* shabby. You'll get settled in no time, I'm sure. BUILD. GOOD. HOUSE.

MRS. SHIMERDA (*"Please help! What can we do?"*): Prosím Vás pomozte! Co máme dělat?

OTTO (*carrying a basket with bread, meat and pies*): Welcome gifts for you!

ÁNTONIA: Ohhhh, much thank!

MRS. SHIMERDA: I . . . *Shimerda.*

GRANDMOTHER: Welcome, Mrs . . . *Shimerda*.

AMBROSCH emerges from the den.

GRANDMOTHER: Well, now who do we have here?

MRS. SHIMERDA: Ahhhh . . . *Ambrosch*.

She flexes her muscles and smacks him on the shoulders to indicate a sturdy constitution.

MRS. SHIMERDA: . . . and *Ántonia*.

GRANDMOTHER: Very nice to meet you. May I see inside, Mrs. Shimerda?

MRS. SHIMERDA, AMBROSCH, and GRANDMOTHER exit. ÁNTONIA reaches coaxingly for JIM's hand.

ÁNTONIA: Pssst!

JIM takes it and they run off together, away from the adults. She races him through the grass. They laugh as they run. They play in the grass. They race to the edge of the bluffs over Squaw Creek, out of breath.

ÁNTONIA *(to JIM)*: Name? What name?

JIM *(carefully)*: I'm Jim.

ÁNTONIA: *Jim. Jim!*

Pointing at the gold trees.

What name?

JIM: What? Oh, the tree? Em . . . that's a . . . cottonwood I guess.

ÁNTONIA looks at him questioningly.

JIM: Cotton-wood.

ÁNTONIA: Cotton-wood.

JIM: Yep, it's a tree.

ÁNTONIA: *Tree.*

ÁNTONIA laughs and then spins her dress, collapses on the grass, drinks in the sky. JIM sits nearby. ÁNTONIA looks at JIM, at the sky, then back at JIM inquiringly.

JIM: Sssskyyy.

ÁNTONIA shakes her head, sits up, points at JIM's eyes.

Jim: Eyes?

ÁNTONIA shakes her head again. Points up.

ÁNTONIA: Ice.

JIM smiles, shakes his head.

ÁNTONIA (*points quickly to sky, then JIM's eyes, then to the sky*): ICE.

> *Pause.*

ÁNTONIA (*Agitated. Points at JIM's eyes, nods*): ICE.

> *Points to the sky, JIM follows with his eyes, then she draws a line back down to JIM's eyes, nods again.*

JIM: Oh, blue! Blue sky!

ÁNTONIA (*laughing, clapping*): Ano! Blue! Blue sky, blue ice!

> *JIM clutches his stomach from laughter.*

JIM: *Eyyyes*, not ice!

> *ÁNTONIA shakes her head. JIM, trying to explain, pretends to be cold, shivers and hugs himself.*

JIM: *Ice . . .* (*Then pointing to his eyes.*) *Eyyyes . . .*

ÁNTONIA: *Eyyyes.*

JIM: Yes!

ÁNTONIA: No iiiiice. (*Mimics shiver.*)

> *They laugh with each other, lay down.*
> *ÁNTONIA points in the tree, then holds up her hands and makes a shadow puppet of a bird. Looks at JIM.*

JIM: Bird.

ÁNTONIA: *Bird.*

ÁNTONIA (*repeating*): Jim. Bird. Cotton-wood. Eyyyyes.

> *ÁNTONIA stands up, holds out her arms and feels the breeze.*

ÁNTONIA (*"How do you say wind?"*): Jak se řekne vítr? (*Makes wind sound.*) Wiiiiiiiiiiiiissssshhhhhh.

JIM: Wind.

ÁNTONIA: Ah, wind! (*"In Czech it is wind"*) Česky je to *vítr*.

JIM: Vitr.

ÁNTONIA (*laughing*): Vitr. (*In Czech: "Yes! I learn English and you learn Czech!"*): Ano! Ja se naučím anglicky a ty česky!

JIM: You speak so fast!

> *ÁNTONIA takes off a silver ring on her middle finger, holds it out to JIM.*

JIM (*admires it. Then*): Ring.

ÁNTONIA shakes head, hands it to him as if to give it to him.

JIM (*for me?*): Give?

ÁNTONIA (*nodding*): Ano.

> *JIM shakes head. ÁNTONIA nods and places ring in his hand, points to him.*

JIM: No, that's yours . . .

ÁNTONIA: Ano!

MR. SHIMERDA (*off*): Ántonia! Ántonia!

JIM: No, I can't—

> *She insists.*

JIM: —No, no, no . . .

> *ÁNTONIA pushes the ring into his hand.*

JIM: NO!

> *Pause.*

MR. SHIMERDA (*off*): Ántonia!

ÁNTONIA (*shouting*): Tatinek, tatinek!

> *MR. SHIMERDA enters. ÁNTONIA runs to him. He is affectionate with her.*

ÁNTONIA (*bringing MR. SHIMERDA to JIM*): My papa. *Tatinek,* his name . . . *Jim.*

> *MR. SHIMERDA smiles. He grabs JIM by the shoulder, looks into his eyes with respect, earnestness.*

ÁNTONIA (*"He is teaching me English words"*): Učí mne anglicky.

MR. SHIMERDA (*"Is he sharp?"*): Je chytrý?

> *She nods.*

GRANDMOTHER (*calling from outside the cave*): Jim! JIM! We need to be on our way!!!

> *MR. SHIMERDA, ÁNTONIA, and JIM begin walking back to the Shimerda cave.*

MR. SHIMERDA (*"Ahhh... You must listen to him—learn English!"*): Aah . . . Musíš ho poslouchat, naučit se anglicky

ÁNTONIA (*"You, too!"*): Ty taky!

MR. SHIMERDA (*"No, I'm not going to learn."*): Ne, já ne!

ÁNTONIA: (*"What? Why not?"*): Cože? Proč ne?

MR. SHIMERDA: (*"I speak Czech."*): Já mluvím česky.

ÁNTONIA (*"Papa! You must learn, too! Maybe you'll find men to play music with."*): Papa Ty taky Třeba najdeš další muzikanty.

> *She makes fiddle playing motions when she says "music."*

MR. SHIMERDA (*"There is no music here."*): Tady muzikanti nejsou.

ÁNTONIA: Papa!

> *MR. SHIMERDA pulls out a small translation dictionary and holds it out to JIM, showing him the pages.*

MR. SHIMERDA: Bohemian. (*Points to opposing page.*) English. (*Hands him the book.*) Te-e-ach, te-e-ach my Ántonia!

> *JIM accepts the book.*

Scene 4: Autumn Lengthens

(*Sound. Workers, including AMBROSCH, create the autumn. They are elevated above the stage working in a way that suggests they're loading a thresher, but it's a "thresher" that sends colors floating to the stage. Work is also suggested by the movement of simple scenery. The SHIMERDAS work about their hovel and slowly close it up to make way for the next scene.*)

NARRATOR JIM: All the years that have passed have not dimmed my memory of that first glorious autumn.

> *ÁNTONIA exits the Shimerda hovel.*

ÁNTONIA: Bye, Papa!

MR. SHIMERDA (*"Ahhhh, there goes my heart . . . Out into the world!"*): Ahh, moje zlato odchází do světa.

NARRATOR JIM: Almost every day Ántonia came running across the prairie to have her reading lesson with me and watch Grandmother in the kitchen.

MRS. SHIMERDA: You learn English, forget Bohemia . . . !

ÁNTONIA (*calling back*): Mamenka, it important for me to learn!

AMBROSCH (*closing up the hovel door, to MR. SHIMERDA*): Tatínku! WORK for fix DOOR!

MRS. SHIMERDA (*to ÁNTONIA*): Go, go . . .

> *ÁNTONIA runs across stage to the Burden farm. OTTO and another worker are just coming down from their afternoon work. JIM and ÁNTONIA sit together. JIM shows her the words in a book.*

JIM: Want to go see the prairie dogs?

ÁNTONIA: And owls!

JIM: Let's go!

ÁNTONIA: Goodbye, Mrs. Burden!

GRANDMOTHER: Careful a' rattlers down there!

JIM: We will!

> JIM and ÁNTONIA run away together. They watch owls returning to earthen homes.

ÁNTONIA: They are wings, but live in prairie dog hole? Under the ground?

JIM: I saw them go down there.

ÁNTONIA: Owls need live high in trees! They like rats.

JIM: Otto says those holes probably go down 200 feet.

ÁNTONIA: Noooo . . .

JIM: Yeah, it's how the prairie dogs get water.

ÁNTONIA: I don't believe it.

JIM: It's true, how else do they drink? There're no ponds—

ÁNTONIA: No—

JIM: —or anything near here!

ÁNTONIA: No. They lick the flowers in morning . . . like this (*indicates licking action*) . . . like rabbits—

JIM: —That's not what Otto said.

ÁNTONIA: Otto not know!

JIM: Yes, he does! He saw prairie dog towns when he worked out in the desert! (*ÁNTONIA laughs.*) He's seen more things than you!

ÁNTONIA (*teasing his hair*): Little Jim.

> JIM pushes her hand away.

JIM: Come *on!* You need more reading practice.

> Light change. They climb up a grassy bank to reach the sunshine. ÁNTONIA shivers.

ÁNTONIA (*as they climb the grassy bank*): In Bohemia, the badger is big prize for mans. They live in holes like prairie dog, but mans send special dog into holes to kill them. Terrific struggle under the ground!

JIM: I bet the rattlesnakes don't struggle much with the prairie dogs . . .

ÁNTONIA: No, that easy!

JIM: They just wait outside and then snap the eggs and puppies!

ÁNTONIA: Easy lunch for them!

>   *She makes a slurping sound.*

JIM: Ugh!

>   *ÁNTONIA laughs. She spies a grasshopper and catches it in her hand.*

ÁNTONIA (*"I caught him!"*): Chytila jsem ji!

JIM: You caught him!

ÁNTONIA (*"grasshopper"*): Kobylka!

JIM: Grass-hopper.

ÁNTONIA: Grass. Hopper.

JIM: I bet he's the last one out here.

ÁNTONIA (*"It's okay, you are okay. I will keep you warm, I will keep you safe . . ."*): Neboj, neboj, já tě zahřeji, ochráním tě.

>   *ÁNTONIA cries.*

JIM: Why are you crying?

ÁNTONIA: At home we have woman called Old Hata. She is . . . beggar, she sell herbs and roots she dig up in the forest . . . and sing to the children in cracky voice like *this*.

>   *Holds up grasshopper. They listen to the rusty chirp. The light slowly changes.*

JIM: Strong little guy.

>   *MR. SHIMERDA enters walking slowly, dragging his feet. He is stooped and moves like his heart and other internal organs have been displaced. Carries a shotgun.*

ÁNTONIA (*jumping up*): Look, my papa! (*Calling out*) Papa!

>   *MR. SHIMERDA waves back. She places the grasshopper in her hair to keep it warm.*

ÁNTONIA: Here, grass-hopper, I make for warm in here.

>   *JIM and ÁNTONIA run across the field to meet him.*

ÁNTONIA: My papa sick all the time, Jim. He not look good. At home he play violin all the time; for weddings and for dance. Such beautiful music. Here never. I beg for him to play and he shake his head *no*. (*To MR. SHIMERDA*) Hello, Papa!

>   *MR. SHIMERDA puts down gun, hugs ÁNTONIA, holds up rabbits. Talks to ÁNTONIA in Czech.*

MR. SHIMERDA (*"Look what I caught us!"*): Podívej co jsem chytnul.

ÁNTONIA: Good, Papa!

MR. SHIMERDA (*"Learning the way! I will make you a hat..."*): Učím se. Udělám ti klobouk.

ÁNTONIA: Aaaaah! Good! (*to JIM*) My *tatinek* make me little hat with the skins, little hat for winter. Meat for eat, skin for hat!

> *JIM examines the gun on ground. MR. SHIMERDA touches ÁNTONIA's hair and she recoils. Speaks rapidly in Czech about the grasshopper and Old Hata. MR. SHIMERDA looks in her hair, we hear the grasshopper chirp. MR. SHIMERDA listens, appears to be in pain. JIM watches him. MR. SHIMERDA opens his eyes, sees JIM with gun.*

MR. SHIMERDA (*"Tell him when he is older the gun is his."*): Ta puška je jeho, až vyroste.

ÁNTONIA: My *tatinek* say when you are big boy he give you his gun. Very fine, from Bohemia. It was belong to great man, very rich, like what you not got here.

JIM: I was just looking.

> *MR. SHIMERDA and ÁNTONIA walk away hand in hand, leaving JIM behind. Evening. We see the SHIMERDAS at home and the BURDENS at home simultaneously. OTTO enters finishing up his work and singing "The Streets of Laredo." GRANDMOTHER enters, sets table.*

OTTO (*singing*): As I walked out on the streets of Laredo,
  As I walked out in Laredo one day,
  I spied a young cowboy, all wrapped in white linen,
  Wrapped in white linen and cold as the clay.

> *GRANDMOTHER takes over humming the tune as OTTO speaks.*

JIM: What happened to your ear?

OTTO: Lost half of it to frostbite. Caught out in a blizzard one night way up in Wyoming when I was helping keep ranch out there. Half the ear turned coal black!

JIM: Really?

OTTO: Yep. Had to cut it off. I can tell you what, that smarted a bit. Can still hear through it, though.

> *As OTTO and GRANDMOTHER continue to sing, we see ÁNTONIA bring the fiddle to MR. SHIMERDA. He declines to play. She places it next to him, crawls in her bed, shivering. MRS. SHIMERDA joins her. AMBROSCH stares at his father.*

OTTO (*singing*): We beat the drum slowly and played the fife lowly,
  And bitterly wept as we bore him along.
  For we loved our comrade, so brave, young and handsome,
  We all loved our comrade, although he'd done wrong.

GRANDFATHER: Prayers, boys.

> *JIM, OTTO, GRANDMOTHER and GRANDFATHER congregate for prayers. MR. SHIMERDA picks up his violin, fingers the strings gently. AMBROSCH and ÁNTONIA watch him.*

GRANDFATHER (*Exodus 35:35*): " . . . Them hath he filled with wisdom of heart, to work all manner of work, of the engraver, and of the skillful workman, and of the embroiderer, in blue, and in scarlet, and in fine linen, and of the weaver, all them that do any work, and of those that devise skillful works." *Amen.*

JIM/OTTO: *Amen.*

SCENE 5: SNAKE IN THE GRASS

(In the blackout, we hear ÁNTONIA calling out excitedly while running.)

ÁNTONIA: *Jim, Jim, Jim! JIM!!! Where are you?!?*

> *Pause.*

JIIIIIIM! Mrs. Buuur-den! HELLO?

> *Lights slowly rise on ÁNTONIA running toward the farmhouse. ÁNTONIA enters like it's her own home.*

ÁNTONIA: Mrs. Burden! Hi, Jim! I have news! Hello!

GRANDMOTHER (*laughing*): Hello, Ántonia!

ÁNTONIA: Hello, Mrs. Burden! I am excite! My papa find friends up north, with Russian mans. Last night he take me for see and I can understand very much talk!

JIM: You mean those two Russian guys up in the cabin?

ÁNTONIA: Yes! You know?

JIM: Just past the dog town?

ÁNTONIA: Yes! Yes!

GRANDMOTHER: Mm-hmm, they've been here a fair set of years. Pavel and Peter.

ÁNTONIA: Yes! Nice mans, Mrs. Burden. One is fat and all the time laugh—

GRANDMOTHER: That would be Peter—

ÁNTONIA: *Everybody* laugh. The first time I see my papa laugh in this kawn-tree. Oh, very nice!

GRANDMOTHER: *Good.*

JIM: They give me chills.

ÁNTONIA: Why "chills"?

JIM: They're so strange! Russia's farther away than China!

ÁNTONIA: Oh, Jim, you not been nowhere in the world.

GRANDMOTHER: Some people say Pavel's an anarchist. They all steer clear of him, but I think he's just an odd fish out of water. Peter they call R-r-r-rooshian Peter! Lord, does that man love his cow. (*Laughs.*) Mr. Burden says those two are good, stout workers.

ÁNTONIA: My papa love them *both.*

GRANDMOTHER: Pavel still sickly?

ÁNTONIA: Oh, yes, he cough very bad.

GRANDMOTHER: They've got Wick Cutter for a creditor. Wicked scoundrel. When they're late paying, their debt grows faster than any crop could possibly . . .

ÁNTONIA: Krajiek cheat them too.

GRANDMOTHER: Poor men.

ÁNTONIA: But funny! We go to see them again tonight!

GRANDMOTHER: It will be good for them to know you.

ÁNTONIA: Jim, I have idea for where we go today.

JIM: Okay.

ÁNTONIA: I think we go in dog town and dig for find out how deep go the holes.

JIM: Sure!

ÁNTONIA: Let's go!

> *They run out together, JIM grabs a spade for digging.*

JIM: I bet they go *straight down—*

ÁNTONIA: I bet they go sideways—!

JIM: Maybe there'll be snakeskins or owl eggs inside!

ÁNTONIA: Or little puppies!

> *They continue to run.*

ÁNTONIA: Over there!

JIM: *Whoa!* This one has two entrances.

> *ÁNTONIA is above JIM while he crawls on the stage floor inspecting the hole.*
> *An actor approaches JIM from behind. He has a long, thick black belt or a whip*

he manipulates to move behind JIM like a snake. ÁNTONIA shrieks out in Czech.

ÁNTONIA (*screams, then "Look out, Jim! Snake!"*): Pozor, Jime! Had!

> *JIM whirls around.*
> *The snake rears back to spring, but JIM rushes in and smashes the snake with his spade. He goes mad with hatred and begins smashing the snake repeatedly and screaming while he does it. Finally, he jumps away.*

ÁNTONIA: Jim! Oh, Jimmy, did he bite you? He not hurt you?

JIM (*yelling*): What did you jabber Bohunk at me for? Are you trying to kill me?

ÁNTONIA: I was scared!

> *She tries to wipe his face with her handkerchief, but he snatches it away.*

JIM: Get out of here!

> *Pause.*

ÁNTONIA: I never knew you was so brave. You is like big mans. Ain't you feel scared a bit? You wait for him to lift his head and then you go for him—!

> *JIM shrugs.*

ÁNTONIA: Let's take him home and show everybody. Nobody ain't never seen in this kawn-tree so big a snake as you kill!

> *ÁNTONIA runs on ahead, JIM drags the snake behind him.*

Everybody! Everybody! Come see what Jim kill! Come see! Hurry, Jim! So slow!

JIM (*laughing*): Wait up!

> *GRANDMOTHER and OTTO emerge. See the snake. GRANDMOTHER shrieks.*

GRANDMOTHER: Jim, drop it! Drop it NOW!

JIM: It's dead . . .

OTTO: Look at that beauty . . .

ÁNTONIA: Jim kill!

GRANDMOTHER: *What?*

OTTO: Where'd you run into *him*?

GRANDMOTHER: Oh, you gave me such a fright!

JIM: Up at the dog-town . . .

OTTO: He fight hard?

ÁNTONIA: He fight something awful! He is all over Jimmy's boots. I scream for him to run, but he just hit and hit that snake like he was crazy.

OTTO (*winking*): Got him the head first crack, huh?

ÁNTONIA: Jim is big fellow now! Big man! Oh, very brave!

> *They examine the snake.*

SCENE 6: THE RUSSIANS' STORY

NARRATOR JIM: While the autumn color was growing pale on the grass and cornfields, things went badly for our Russian friends. Pavel strained himself lifting timbers for a new barn, and fell over among the shavings with a gush of blood from the lungs.

> One evening soon after, Pavel asked for Mr. Shimerda and Ántonia, who had become his close friends. I accompanied.

> *ÁNTONIA, MR. SHIMERDA, and JIM travel during NARRATOR JIM's speech. They enter the Russians's cabin as it concludes. PAVEL is lying in bed, dying. PAVEL lies in the center of the stage in dim light. MR. SHIMERDA sits by, rubbing the man's legs to soothe him. They talk quietly to each other.*

ÁNTONIA (*whispering*): He is very bad, Jim. Very bad off.

JIM: He can hardly breathe.

> *The sounds of distant coyotes are heard. PAVEL gasps and attempts to sit up. He begins whispering. The coyotes increase their howls then begin yapping. PAVEL struggles with MR. SHIMERDA and whispers frantically.)*

ÁNTONIA (*to JIM, a whisper*): He is scared of the wolves. In his country . . . there are many . . . (*gasps*) and they eat men and women.

> *PAVEL tells his story. He is whispering so that he is barely audible. His rapid breathing and occasional exhalations punctuate the action of the story. His whispers and breaths should make their own language or music during the telling of the tale. ÁNTONIA listens and translates. As she does, the lights slowly dim so only PAVEL and ÁNTONIA are lit.*

ÁNTONIA: It's awful what he says . . . !

JIM (*whispering*): What is it?

> *ÁNTONIA listens.*

ÁNTONIA: When Pavel and Peter were young men in Russia . . . they have honor to be *mládenci* for friend who was to marry pretty girl in other village. It was *uprostred zimy*—very much snow on fields—and the *ženich* party went over to the wedding in *sáně*, eh . . . *sáně*, is . . . um, wintertime . . . uh, sledges. They go in *sledges*.

> At midnight after the party is over, the *ženich* he carry his bride in his arms to his *sáně*—his, his *sledges*. Pavel drive the horse. The party was singing and

there was happy sound of the bells . . . the *ženich* sledge go first over the dark snow.

First they hear one wolf-cry, but the drivers are not much afraid. They too happy and have too much drink. The wolf sounds come fast and near. There no moon in sky, but the stars make light on snow. The wolves are like shadow; there so many of them . . . hundreds. Hundreds of wolves.

Something happen to the sledge far in back: the driver lose hold and the sledge overturn. The people roll out over the snow, and the wolves jump on them. The screaming make everyone cold. The drivers lash their horses.

Another driver lose hold. The screaming of the horses are more terrible to hear than cries of the men and women. Nothing stop the wolves. *Nothing.*

The *ženich* scream. He see his *tatinek* sledge turn over, with his *mamenka* and sisters. He try to jump. But, his bride hold him. Then Pavel have idea.

PAVEL's breathing becomes desperate. Shallow, painful, noisy intakes of air.

Pavel step into the back of the sledge. He call to the *ženich*—his friend—that they must . . . lighten—and he point to the bride. His friend spit at him and hold her tight. Pavel try to drag her away. They fight and Pavel knock him over side of the sledge and then . . . pick up and throw the girl after him. Then. They hear new sound. Louder than ever before . . . It is the bell of the church of their own village, ringing for early prayer.

PAVEL convulses, his whole body reaching up, straining.

Pavel and Peter drive into village alone, and they . . . are . . . alone ever since. They are run out of their village. Pavel's own *mamenka* not look at him. They go away to strange towns, but when people learn where they from, they always ask if they know two men who feed bride to wolves. They work in Chicago, Des Moines, Fort Wayne, but they were always bad luck.

PAVEL dies.
MR. SHIMERDA listens for breath, then stands. On NARRATOR JIM's next lines, he walks slowly toward the audience, almost as though he will walk over their heads. He exits through the audience.

NARRATOR JIM: After Pavel died, Peter sold off everything, and left the county. Mr. Shimerda had lost his two only friends.

The merciless Black Hawk money-lender who held mortgages on their livestock, including Peter's beloved cow, brought in the sale notes for dirt cheap.

WICK CUTTER enters. Picks up the bench PAVEL was lying on as he died, carries it off.

Wick Cutter. More on him later.

CUTTER exits.
JIM and ÁNTONIA, holding hands, both exit slowly into the darkness.

Scene 7: Winter in the Soul

(The workers create a thick, beautiful snowfall. They are working in freezing conditions, like Arctic explorers. As they do, JIM drives ÁNTONIA in an old horse-drawn sleigh over the countryside. Enchanting sound.)

JIM: LOOK AT IT!

ÁNTONIA (*"The snow changes the whole world!"*): Sníh mění celý svět!

JIM: What was that?

ÁNTONIA: The snow changes the whole world!

JIM: It does!

ÁNTONIA: Beautiful!

JIM: Keep going?

ÁNTONIA: Yes! I never want to go back to that hole again! *Mamenka* is awful! I want to scream at her!

JIM: We can't sled forever! The wind is picking up!

ÁNTONIA: Anything would be better!

> The sleigh comes to a halt, they jump off into the snow, laughing, say goodbye. They return to their separate homes.

OTTO (*entering farmhouse with JIM*): Saw Ambrosch today out in the fields. He was dragging a bundle of prairie dogs he shot.

GRANDFATHER: What's he doing with those?

OTTO: Bringing 'em home for food he said.

GRANDMOTHER: Josiah, you don't suppose Shimerda would let them eat prairie dog, do you?

GRANDFATHER: Not sure. If a body's hungry enough.

OTTO: I told him he didn't want to go eating those, but he just grinned like he was smarter than me.

JIM: What do they taste like?

OTTO: Not sure any of us knows.

GRANDMOTHER: I think we ought to pay the Shimerdas a visit, don't you? It's been weeks since we've seen any of them.

JIM: You can eat them, though?

OTTO: Not sure if you'd want to. Their blood lines are against them in that department.

GRANDFATHER: A visit sounds like a good idea.

JIM: How?

OTTO: Part of the rat family.

JIM: Ew!

GRANDFATHER: That's enough, Otto.

> (*The hovel is revealed in filthy, ragged condition. The SHIMERDAS appear broken and torn apart each in their own way. They are grotesque. They are all wearing rags on their raw feet. When GRANDMOTHER enters, MRS. SHIMERDA's cries cut the air.*)
>
> *JIM and GRANDMOTHER enter.*

MRS. SHIMERDA (*sobbing; "Ohhhh, help us! Help us! Look at my feet, they are swaddled in rags. I can't feel my fingers and we are all so hungry! HELP US!!!"*): Ohh, pomozte nám, pomozte nám! Moje nohy, necítím prsty . . . všichni máme hlad. POMOZTE!

> *She pulls the top off a barrel and pulls them over to look inside.*

MRS. SHIMERDA (*in English*): Look! Nothing! Rotten! Rotten! None left! Not even scrap!

GRANDMOTHER (*murmuring*): Yes, I see. It's not much . . .

> *MRS. SHIMERDA cackles scornfully. Seizes an old tin can with bits of metal in it and shakes it at GRANDMOTHER and then at JIM, frightening him.*

GRANDMOTHER: Very tough times, Mrs. Shimerda. Winter is a devil . . .

> *OTTO enters with a food hamper. MR. SHIMERDA stands.*

OTTO: Suppertime!

> *MRS. SHIMERDA breaks down. She falls and sobs at GRANDMOTHER's feet.*

ÁNTONIA (*whispering*): You not mind my poor *mamenka*, Mrs. Burden. She is so sad.

GRANDMOTHER: No, dear, not at all. (*They unpack a basket.*) Haven't you got a cave or cellar outside, Ántonia? How did the potatoes get frozen?

ÁNTONIA: We get from Mr. Bushy at the post office—what he throw out. We got no potatoes of our own . . .

> *MR. SHIMERDA places his hand on GRANDMOTHER's arm. He draws her over to a hole in the wall and points at the blankets inside.*

MR. SHIMERDA: My Ántonia!

GRANDMOTHER (*after a beat*): You mean she sleeps in there?

> MR. SHIMERDA *nods.* ÁNTONIA *exits quickly.* JIM *follows her into the cold.*

ÁNTONIA (*after a beat*): I don't mind to sleep in that hole. At least it warm!

> *Pause.*

My *mamenka* say "Burdens are selfish," but then here you is tonight. (*Sad laugh.*) My papa is so sad. He don't like this kawn-tree.

JIM: People who don't like this country ought to stay at home.

ÁNTONIA: He not want to come, ne-ver! My *mamenka* make him come. My papa he cry for leave his old friends what make music with him. But my mama, she want Ambrosch for be rich—for *Ambrosch* we come.

JIM: Your mother wants other people's things.

ÁNTONIA: Your grandpa is rich, why he no help my papa?

> *Pause.*

ÁNTONIA: I ask my papa to play fiddle for me for Christmas.

JIM: What'd he say?

> *Blast of howling wind and snowfall and sound. The beginning of a blizzard.*

Scene 8: Testament

(A spot appears. The sound of wind continues. MR. SHIMERDA talks to us.)

MR. SHIMERDA: We were not beggars in the old country. We were happy. Our stomachs and our souls were never hungry, never. I made good wages as a weaver. My work was beautiful. I worked with the finest cloth. I miss the feeling of silk on my fingers.

My family was respected. *I* was respected. We were not looked upon the way we are here.

Oh, I used to love to play music. At weddings, in the city square . . . My best friend—his name was Tomek—he play the, what's the name for it in English . . . ?

> *Here MR. SHIMERDA attempts to ask an audience member the name of the trombone. He shows how a trombone is played by indicating the slide action and makes the sound of the trombone with his mouth. He asks, "Please? In English?" An audience member says, "Trombone."*

MR. SHIMERDA (*in English*): Yes! Trom-Bone! Thank you!

We used to make music and I'd lose myself. I'd forget where I was while we played. My bow sawed my fiddle on its own.

When we left Bohemia, the Shimerdas had over a thousand dollars. After the passage fee was paid! But, then, we lost some in New York and then the rail fare to Nebraska cost much more than we expected . . . And then Krajiek. By the time we were done paying him for the mud cave and the broken animals and rusty machinery, well! We had little money left! To think . . . he is Czech and he comes here, over the ocean on a filthy ship like us . . . and then saps the blood out of people from his very own land. What kind of creature does that?

I still have some money. Ambrosch and Ántonia will do well. They're both old enough to work the fields. I had other dreams for my Ántonia . . . But she is willing to work. She says that. They can plant a garden. Buy new animals. They will do well.

Enough with this winter! The logs we chopped for our new house are *frozen* through! Buried!

My daughter sleeps in an earthen hole dug into the wall of our cave. My Ántonia! My *daughter*.

He exits. Blackout.

SCENE 9: PRAIRIE OF THE SHADOW

GRANDMOTHER (*a cry in the dark*): Oh, dear Saviour! Lord, Thou knowest!

> (*GRANDFATHER's voice is heard, muffled. He's asking questions: "I need you to tell me exactly what happened as it happened, or what you know from what you heard . . ." Slow fade up to a stage completely white. JIM is waking up. OTTO, GRANDMOTHER, GRANDFATHER, and a strange man lying asleep in the corner are all congregated in the kitchen.*)

GRANDFATHER: Get up, Jim! Get up! We have work to do. NOW, son! Let's go—at the table!

JIM: What about prayers?

GRANDFATHER: We won't be having prayers this morning . . .

JIM: Why?

GRANDFATHER: Old Mr. Shimerda is dead—

JIM: *What?*—

GRANDFATHER: —and his family are in great distress.

JIM: How? What happened?

GRANDMOTHER: Oh, Lord!

GRANDFATHER: Otto and Ambrosch have been up all night in the snow, so leave them be. Come on in to breakfast. Otto?

OTTO: Sir.

GRANDFATHER: Did anybody hear the gun go off?

OTTO: No, sir. Ambrosch says he was out with the ox team, trying to break a road and the women-folks was shut up tight in their cave—

GRANDFATHER: But, what . . . preceded this?

OTTO: Ambrosch says when he come in, the oxen acted kinda queer. One of 'em ripped around and got away from him—bolted clean out of the stable.

GRANDMOTHER: Poor soul! He was always so un-wishful to give us trouble. How could he forget himself like this?!?

OTTO: From what I seen he wasn't outta his head for a minute, Mrs. Burden. It was all done natural.

GRANDFATHER: How "natural?"

OTTO: You know he was sorta fixy and that's how he was right to the end.

JIM: What's fixy?

GRANDFATHER: *JIM.*

OTTO: Well, you know. Sorta . . . fine . . . a . . . gentleman.

GRANDFATHER: Yes, he was.

GRANDMOTHER: Poor man—

OTTO: He shaved after dinner, and washed hisself all over after the girls had done the dishes. Ántonia heated the water for him . . .

GRANDMOTHER: Good Lord, what *she* must be *feeling* right now . . .

OTTO: He put on a clean shirt and socks, that silk neckcloth he always wore. He kissed Ántonia, took his gun, and told them he was going out to hunt some rabbits. He musta gone right to the barn and done it then. He laid down on that bunk-bed, close to the ox stalls, where he slept.

> AMBROSCH, *the figure in the corner, stirs, sits up. He pulls out a rosary and prays slavishly in Czech. His fervently whispered prayers are amplified.*

GRANDMOTHER: I don't see how he could do it!

OTTO: Well, ma'am, it was simple enough—he pulled the trigger with his big toe. He laid over on his side and put the end of the barrel in his mouth, then he drew up one foot and felt for the trigger. He found it alright!

GRANDFATHER: Krajiek see him like that?

OTTO: Sure did. He begun to squeal like a rat and run about wringing his hands. Kept saying "They'll hang me, they'll hang me."

GRANDFATHER: Huh.

OTTO: If I hadn't seen bunches of hair and stuff sticking to the poles and straw along the roof, I'd'a thought Krajiek killed him, the way he was acting.

GRANDMOTHER: Ghastly. Just *ghastly*. Josiah, I mean to go to the Shimerdas' with you when you go.

GRANDFATHER: There's nothing for you to do. The body can't be touched before the coroner gets here from Black Hawk.

GRANDMOTHER: Well, I can sure bring them some victuals, anyway, and try to comfort that poor girl. He might've thought of her! She was his *darling*.

OTTO: I'll get going to get the priest and coroner.

> MR. SHIMERDA, *finely dressed, enters, fiddle in hand. JIM sees him. He walks around, content and happy, looking at the house and the scene before him. AMBROSCH's whispers continue.*

GRANDMOTHER: Now, how are you going to make it there in this weather, Otto?

OTTO: Don't worry about me, Mrs. Burden, I've got a good nose for directions. It'll work the gelding hard, though, this weather.

GRANDFATHER: Do the best you can for yourself.

> OTTO, GRANDFATHER AND GRANDMOTHER *exit.* MR. SHIMERDA *lifts his violin to his chin, begins to play. No sound comes out, but as he saws the bow,* AMBROSCH's *whispered prayers become very loud.* JIM *sits.* AMBROSCH *stops praying at the same moment* MR. SHIMERDA *stops playing. They exit, leaving* JIM *alone on stage.*

NARRATOR JIM: On the day of the funeral, Otto and Grandfather went ahead to cut Mr. Shimerda's body from the pool of blood in which he was frozen.

ÁNTONIA (*running to him*): Oh, Jim, what you think for my lovely Papa?

> *They embrace.*

GRANDFATHER: Great and Just God, no man knows what the sleeper knows, nor is it for us to judge what lies between him and Thee. If any man living in Your Creation has been remiss toward the stranger come to a far country, we ask that You forgive him and soften his heart. We pray, Good Lord, for this man's widow and his now fatherless children and we ask you to smooth the way before them and to incline the hearts of men to deal justly with them. We leave him, Lord, at Thy judgment seat, which is also Thy mercy seat. *Amen.*

ALL: *Amen.*

> JIM *and* ANTONIA *still holding each other.* OTTO *sings "Bury Me Not On the Lonesome Prairie" or "Jesus, Lover of my Soul."*

NARRATOR JIM (*over OTTO's singing*): Years afterward, when the red grass had been ploughed under until it had almost disappeared from the prairie, Mr. Shimerda's grave was still there, with a sagging wire fence around it, and an unpainted wooden cross. In all that country it was the spot most dear to me. Never a tired driver passed that site, I am sure, without wishing well to the sleeper.

SCENE 10: RELEASED FROM WINTER'S JAWS

(*Spring is created, this time by ÁNTONIA, who is directed incessantly by AMBROSCH while he works. The stage should be changed somehow to suggest renewal as the dawn of spring does.*)

JIM (*calling out to ÁNTONIA while she works*): Hi, Tony!

ÁNTONIA: HI, JIM!

JIM: I was just over at the Iverson's catalpa groves—

ÁNTONIA: No time to talk, Jimmy! Work to do!

NARRATOR JIM: Since winter I had seen very little of Ántonia. She was out in the fields from sunup until sundown.

> JIM goes to sit. ÁNTONIA comes in from work at dusk.

ÁNTONIA (*sitting, fanning herself*): Oooof, so much plough today! Ambrosch on the north quarter for break sod all day. Tough job!

JIM: I saw him out there.

ÁNTONIA: You see that big prairie fire last night, Jim? Your grandpa lose stacks?

JIM: I don't think so.

ÁNTONIA: Oh, good. Ambrosch say prices good this year!

JIM: Tony, Grandmother wants to know if you're going to go to school. A new term starts next week over at the sod schoolhouse.

ÁNTONIA: For me?

JIM (*nodding*): She says there's a new teacher and you'd learn a lot.

> ÁNTONIA stands.

ÁNTONIA: I ain't got time to learn. I work like mans now.

JIM: But, you could—

ÁNTONIA: Mother can't say no more how Ambrosch do all and nobody to help him.

JIM: *I'm going*—

ÁNTONIA: I can work as much as him. (*Flexes arm.*) You feel my muscle?

> *She turns away toward home. JIM follows.*

JIM: School is—

ÁNTONIA: School is all right for little boys! I help make this land good farm.

JIM: *I thought you wanted to go to school!*

ÁNTONIA: I DON'T!

> *ÁNTONIA stops. She is crying.*

Sometime you tell me some things you learn at school. Okay?

JIM: Sure . . .

ÁNTONIA: My father went very much to school . . . He read so many books the priests in Bohemia come talk to him!

> *She laughs at the thought.*

ÁNTONIA: You no forget my papa?

JIM: How could I?

MRS. SHIMERDA (*calling from inside, "Ántonia! Get in here! Supper! Ask Jim to stay too."*): Ántonia, pojd' sem Večeře At' Jim taky přijde.

ÁNTONIA: Okay, *mamenka*!

> *They enter house.*

MRS. SHIMERDA: Jim. When your grandfather begin plant corn?

JIM: Well, he says earlier this year than last.

MRS. SHIMERDA: Yes?

JIM: Yeah, he says we should have a dry spring, so the corn won't be held back by rain like last year . . . Planting should be pretty smooth.

MRS. SHIMERDA (*scoffing*): He not Jesus. He not know about the wet and the dry.

> *AMBROSCH laughs. ÁNTONIA eats noisily.*

ÁNTONIA: Jim, you ask Otto how much he plough today. I don't want that Otto get more done than me. I *strong* now. I want we have very much corn this fall.

AMBROSCH: I plough more than you today . . .

MRS. SHIMERDA (*pointing at AMBROSCH, egging ÁNTONIA on*): Oooohhh . . . !

> *AMBROSCH and ÁNTONIA dispute briefly in Czech, MRS. SHIMERDA enjoying it.*

AMBROSCH: You take them ox tomorrow and try the sod plough. Then you not be so smart, goose liver!

MRS. SHIMERDA laughs.

ÁNTONIA: Don't be mad, Ambrožíčku . . . You want I milk the cow for you tomorrow?

MRS. SHIMERDA (*scoffing again*): That cow not give us so much milk like your grandfather say.

AMBROSCH (*accusatory*): Pbbbbt! Only little drops!

MRS. SHIMERDA: If he make talk about fifteen dollars I owe, I send him back the cow . . .

JIM: He doesn't talk about the fifteen dollars! He doesn't find fault with people!

AMBROSCH: He say I break his saw when we build, and I never.

ÁNTONIA hacks up some phlegm.

JIM (*standing*): Thank you for supper, Mrs. Shimerda. I must go now.

MRS. SHIMERDA laughs, waves. AMBROSCH whispers meanly in Czech to MRS. SHIMERDA as JIM exits. ÁNTONIA follows.

ÁNTONIA: Hey! Why you go, Jim?

JIM: I saw him break that saw and I saw him hide it and lie about it!

ÁNTONIA: Ambrosch work very hard now. He bone tired. He forget!

JIM: I have to go home.

(Walks away toward home. As he does, ÁNTONIA turns and begins to work outside. Soon AMBROSCH joins her, he begins rudely commanding her about in Czech. She works harder and harder during the following. It's a new day.)

NARRATOR JIM: As the spring went on, things between me and the Shimerdas grew strained.

GRANDMOTHER: Heavy field work'll spoil that girl!

OTTO: Ooooh, boy, you ought to hear what the boys around the country say about her!

GRANDMOTHER: I'm sure I don't want to know, Otto.

GRANDFATHER: She'll get along in the world before those boys do . . .

GRANDMOTHER: I *miss* having her about.

OTTO: Jim hasn't been visiting them, I notice.

GRANDFATHER: Otto, I'll need you and Jim to retrieve some items from Ambrosch if you would.

OTTO: Sure thing.

JIM and OTTO approach AMBROSCH who is elevated, working on his family's windmill.

JIM: Hey, Ambrosch!

AMBROSCH: Yuh.

JIM: Grandfather wants the horse collar he lent you back.

AMBROSCH (*climbing down, then scratching his head*): Horse collar? Hmmm . . .

JIM: Come on, Ambrosch, I know you have it. If you ain't going to look for it, I will.

AMBROSCH: I get it . . .

He returns carrying a ratty old thing.

AMBROSCH: This what you want?

JIM: That's not the harness Grandfather loaned you, Ambrosch! I can't carry that thing back to him!

AMBROSCH (*throwing harness on the ground at his feet*): All right.

He begins climbing the windmill. JIM loses his temper, runs to AMBROSCH, grabs him by the belt and yanks him down. AMBROSCH hits ground and lunges out at JIM with a vicious kick. JIM punches AMBROSCH on the head and runs.

OTTO: Jim!

ÁNTONIA and MRS. SHIMERDA come running.

ÁNTONIA: Stop it! Stop it!

MRS. SHIMERDA: Law! Law for knock my Ambrosch down!

JIM: Let's get out of here, Otto.

They climb on the wagon, begin to ride off.

ÁNTONIA (*calling after him*): I never like you no more, Jim Burden! NO FRIENDS ANY MORE!

JIM (*yelling back*): You're a damned ungrateful lot! After everything my grandpa's done for you! (*To OTTO*) You hear them!?! After all we went through on account of them last winter! You can't trust 'em!

OTTO: You can't tell me nothing new about a Czech, boy; I'm an Austrian.

JIM: I'll never be friends with them again!

Lights shift.

NARRATOR JIM: It was Grandfather who brought about a reconciliation with the Shimerdas. He wouldn't stand for strife between neighbors for too long.

GRANDFATHER: Emmaline! Jim! Otto! Can I have a word with you?

> *They enter.*

The grain's coming in so well, I think I'll be cutting the first of July. That's soon, and I'm going to need more men. If it's agreeable to everyone here, I'm going to ask Ambrosch to help.

> *Looks squarely at JIM.*

JIM: Yes, sir.

GRANDFATHER: Emmaline, I think I'll ask Ántonia to come over to help in the kitchen if you'd like. She may be happy to earn something.

GRANDMOTHER: With her here we'll all be happy.

Scene 11: Summer Storm

NARRATOR JIM: July came on with that breathless, brilliant heat which makes the plains of Kansas and Nebraska the best corn country in the world. It seemed as if we could hear the corn growing in the night.

ÁNTONIA: Jim, look! Down at the edge of the rows!

NARRATOR JIM: Those July nights, I loved having Ántonia nearby.

> *JIM watches for a moment.*

JIM: Lightning.

ÁNTONIA: Ohhhh . . .

JIM: Coming closer. Want to climb up?

ÁNTONIA: Yes!

> *They climb up to the top of a shack to watch the lightning on the horizon.*

JIM: I keep having dreams about Pavel.

ÁNTONIA: You do?

JIM (*nodding*): It always gets dark fast like this. In the dreams.

ÁNTONIA: What happens?

JIM: I'm always on a sledge drawn by three horses and we're . . . dashing through a country that looks like Nebraska, but somehow is also Virginia.

ÁNTONIA: Scary!

JIM: Have you ever told anyone his secret?

ÁNTONIA: No. Have you?

JIM: No.

> *Pause.*

GRANDMOTHER (*calling up to them*): Jim! Ántonia! Come on down, now, it's late. You'll get wet out there!

ÁNTONIA (*calling back*): In a minute we come!

> *Pause.*

ÁNTONIA: I like your grandmother.

JIM: She likes you.

ÁNTONIA: I like all things here.

JIM: I know. Me too.

ÁNTONIA: Oh, I wish my papa live to see this summer. He love lightning!

> *Pause.*

I wish no winter ever come again.

JIM: It will be summer a long time . . .

> *Pause.*

Why aren't you always nice like this, Tony?

ÁNTONIA: How "nice?"

JIM: Just like this . . . like . . . yourself. Why do you always try to act like Ambrosch?

ÁNTONIA: I like to work out of doors! I don't care if it make me like mans! I have big muscle now!

JIM: I know. That's not what I mean.

ÁNTONIA: You don't know.

JIM: Know what?

ÁNTONIA (*choosing her words carefully*): If I live here, like you, that is different. Things will be easy for you. Always easy. But they will be hard for us.

> *Pause.*
> *Flash of lightning.*

Oh! You see that one?

JIM: Gee, the whole sky cracked!

> *Blackout.*

ACT II

ADOLESCENCE

Scene 1: Welcome to Black Hawk

(Piano music, as heard from an open window.)

NARRATOR JIM: I had been living with my grandfather and grandmother for three years when we moved to Black Hawk, a clean, well-planted little prairie town. The grandparents were getting old for the heavy work of a farm, and as I was now thirteen, they thought I ought to be in school.

> *JIM enters, carrying his books. He's walking home, older now. SALLY and CHARLEY HARLING run up behind him. CHARLEY sneaks up on JIM, but at the last moment, JIM spins around. This is part of a game continued from the school day.*

JIM (*stamping CHARLEY's foot*): RIFTER DRIFTER!

CHARLEY: No!

SALLY: Ohhhhhhh! He got you!

CHARLEY: How did you hear me?!?

JIM: You were louder than a bull coming up behind me!

NARRATOR JIM: It wasn't long before we felt like town people. I was quite another boy, or thought I was, and I played often with our next door neighbor's children.

> *SALLY sneaks up and stamps JIM's foot.*

SALLY: RIFTER DRIFTER!

JIM (*laughing*): Hey! Goddamit!

CHARLEY: Haha! She got you!

MRS. HARLING: James Burden! What did I just hear you say?

JIM (*over his shoulder*): Sorry!

They exit chasing each other.

NARRATOR JIM: All through that first spring and summer, I hoped Ambrosch would bring Ántonia to see our new house. He never did.

JIM, CHARLEY and SALLY run back in, out of breath.

CHARLEY: Okay, okay, no more . . .

They fall to walking. CHARLEY suddenly tries to stomp JIM, but JIM catches him.

JIM (*laughing*): I KNEW IT!

The boys spar with hands locked, they wrestle each other to the ground.

NARRATOR JIM: We heard that he hired her out like a man, worked her too hard, and she went from farm to farm binding sheaves and working with the threshers.

CHARLEY: I GIVE UP!

JIM: Ring king winner!

CHARLEY: No!

JIM: Ow! Dammit!

MRS. HARLING: James Burden! *WATCH YOUR MOUTH.* Charley, Sally, get inside, we've got work to do before supper.

JIM and CHARLEY separate. CHARLEY and SALLY run inside, JIM follows, but is stopped by MRS. HARLING.

MRS. HARLING: What'd I say about your language?

JIM: Sorry.

MRS. HARLING: Keep it up and I won't have you over to the house any more. I mean it—I've got my eye on you.

JIM: Yes, ma'am. Uh, can I go?

MRS. HARLING: Go ahead.

JIM runs into the HARLINGS' house after the kids. Piano music continues, louder. MRS. HARLING and the kids go to work creating the house. This should convey the energy of the line—"House cleaning was like a revolution."

NARRATOR JIM: Grandmother often said that if she had to live in town, she thanked God she lived next to the Harlings.

MRS. HARLING: Wash up for supper, children! Jim, I expect you'll be staying?

JIM: Sure!

NARRATOR JIM: They were Norwegian and had been farming people, like ourselves. Mr. Harling was the most enterprising businessman in our county and Mrs. Harling was a jovial, energetic force of her own.

MRS. HARLING (*calling off*): That's enough, Julia. Wash up. You can play after supper. (*Piano music stops.*) Last meal before our new girl arrives! She'll be here in the morning!

> *Children cheer.*

NARRATOR JIM: When fall came, Grandmother saved Ántonia by getting her work keeping house for the Harlings.

ÁNTONIA (*running on*): HEY Jim!

JIM: Hi!

> *She gives him a light, playful punch on the shoulder.*

ÁNTONIA: You ain't forget about me?

JIM: No!

ÁNTONIA: No?

> *She jabs him again, she's bouncing around.*

JIM: Stop it! No!

ÁNTONIA (*looking about the house*): Wow. Look at this place! Maybe your grandmother like me better now I come to town!

JIM: What? Didn't Ambrosch make you bring a plough to work in your spare time . . . ?

ÁNTONIA: Ooooh, that's a good idea. I keep my muscles.

> *She doubles back and jabs him again, they fall to laughing and the others join them.*
> *Piano music again. ÁNTONIA, MRS. HARLING, and the children sing a joyous evening song with each other. The song gets silly as they sing, SALLY begins playing a game with ÁNTONIA. ÁNTONIA becomes a bear and roars. All the children including JIM run off screaming as she gives chase. MRS. HARLING laughs. Piano music continues.*

CHILDREN: BEAR!!!

MRS. HARLING (*shouting to JULIA offstage*): Nice playing, Julia!

JULIA (*off*): Thank you, Mother!

MRS. HARLING: Chopin?

JULIA: Yes!

SALLY (*running on*): Mother, Ántonia is a bear coming down from the mountain to get us! How do we stop her?

MRS. HARLING (*laughing*): You must be a bigger bear, dear!

> *MRS. HARLING roars. SALLY joins in and roars hugely at ÁNTONIA who stops in place, does a silly scared bear noise and falls down. They all fall to laughing.*

CHARLEY: I feel like some cake!

ÁNTONIA (*stopping playing*): Oh, you do? Um, what kind?

> *She goes to make a cake, JIM and SALLY follow taunting.*

JIM (*whispering*): Sally!

JIM/SALLY: Ohhhhhh . . . "I won't have none of your weevily wheat, and I won't have none of your barley, But I'll take a measure of fine white flour, to make a cake for *Charley* . . ."

ÁNTONIA: *Very funny . . .*

SALLY: You faaaancy him.

> *A knock on the door. The noise dies down, piano stops.*

ÁNTONIA: I'll answer it!

> *She opens the door. LENA LINGARD in elegant town clothes—hat, coat, stockings.*

LENA: Hi, Tony.

> *Pause.*

  Do you know who I am?

ÁNTONIA: Why . . . Lena! You're all . . . *dressed up!*

> *LENA laughs.*

LENA (*waving*): Hello, Jim. Charley.

JIM: Hi.

CHARLEY: Hi.

ÁNTONIA: Well.

> *Pause.*

ÁNTONIA: Well, so! What are you doing here?

LENA: I'm in town now. Got a job to work, too.

ÁNTONIA: Wow, ain't that funny!

LENA: Why, funny?

> *Pause.*

MRS. HARLING: Ántonia? Who's at the door?

ÁNTONIA: Um.

MRS. HARLING: Well . . . show her in . . .

ÁNTONIA: Oh! Oh. Of course.

ÁNTONIA shows LENA in to where MRS. HARLING sits. CHARLEY and SALLY exit.

LENA: Hello.

ÁNTONIA: Mrs. Harling, this is Lena.

Pause.

MRS. HARLING: Lena Lingard?

LENA: Yes.

MRS. HARLING: Hm.

Pause.

MRS. HARLING: So, you've come to town. Are you working?

LENA: For Mrs. Thomas. She's going to teach me to sew. She says I have a knack for it, so . . .

MRS. HARLING: Oh.

LENA: It's gonna be perfect. I'm done with the farm. There ain't any end to work there. It's awful! I decided: I'm going to be a dressmaker.

MRS. HARLING: Well, it's a good trade. There have to be dressmakers, of course. But I wouldn't run down the farm, if I were you.

Pause.

MRS. HARLING: How is your mother?

LENA: Oh, mother's never very well; she works too hard. I'm going to make all sorts of money and send it to her.

MRS. HARLING: See that you don't forget to.

LENA: I won't.

ÁNTONIA: I thought you were going to be married, Lena. To Nick Svendson, wasn't it?

LENA: Ugh. No. I don't want to marry Nick, or any other man. I don't want to ask leave of *anybody*.

MRS. HARLING: Well, I hope you keep your head about you now. Don't go gadding off to dances and neglect your work, the way some country girls do when they get here.

LENA: Yes'm. Oh, Tony, guess what? Tiny Soderball's coming to town, too. She's going to be working at the Boys' Hotel.

MRS. HARLING: Not a good place for a girl. Too many strangers.

LENA: Imagine.

>   *Pause.*

LENA: I guess I'd better be going.

MRS. HARLING: Well. Come again if you're ever lonesome.

LENA: Oh, I don't think I'll ever get lonesome here. Bye, Mrs. Harling.

>   *Exiting through kitchen.*

LENA (*whispering*): I've got a room of my own at Mrs. Thomas's. Meet me there on Saturday night, Tony, we'll go out.

ÁNTONIA: Um. I'll see if I can. Mrs. Harling don't really like me, you know, running about too much.

LENA: What? Can't you do what you want when you're off? Ain't you just crazy about town?

ÁNTONIA (*laughing*): Okay, *bye,* Lena.

LENA: Bye, Tony! Bye, Jim.

JIM: Bye . . .

>   *JIM watches her go off from where he sits.*
>   *Silence.*
>   *ÁNTONIA begins to hum.*

MRS. HARLING: Ántonia, you weren't yourself while Lena was here.

ÁNTONIA: No.

MRS. HARLING: Why?

ÁNTONIA: Oh. I don't know how you feel about her coming 'round. She sort of was talked about in the country and, I don't know, it's funny . . .

MRS. HARLING: Yes. She was talked about here, too.

Scene 2: Jim and Lena on the Street

NARRATOR JIM: Winter comes down savagely over a little town on the prairie. In the bleakness a hunger for color comes over people. After Lena came to town, I often met her downtown.

>   *The street in town. Late fall. JIM walking.*

LENA: Jim!

JIM: Oh, hi.

LENA: Hi. Walking home?

JIM: Yeah. You?

LENA: Oh, no, I'm off to pick up some sewing silk.

JIM: You go on your own?

LENA: Yes, Mrs. Thomas trusts my eye already. I'm good, too. Last week I made my third dress. I love it.

JIM: I'd love to see it.

> She smiles.
> They walk.

LENA: Some of those salesmen have the most exciting life. I hear their stories at the Boys' Hotel when I visit Tiny Saturday nights. I told Ántonia I hope you're a traveling man when you grow up.

JIM: I never really thought about it.

LENA: *Imagine*: riding the rails all day long, seeing theatre in the cities!

JIM: Maybe I will.

LENA: Only thing is, you have to promise to bring me with.

> She winks at him.

LENA: Oh, here's our grand bazaar. (*They laugh.*) Bye, Jim! See you around again!

JIM: Bye.

> She exits, he shoves his hand in his pockets, gets cold. Runs to the HARLINGS' house.
> Piano music, lights, noise, fun. They are finishing up a game of charades.

ÁNTONIA: Oh, this place is like heaven, Mrs. Harling! Pure heaven!

MRS. HARLING (*laughing*): I'm glad!

ÁNTONIA: No Ambrosch sitting around (*imitates Ambrosch, drawing laughter*)— "*Tomorrow you bring back money to me! You work way I say! Unnngggg! Unnnggg!*" I swear, Mrs. Harling, I couldn't stand it no more!

MRS. HARLING: I'm sure they miss you, Ántonia.

ÁNTONIA: I know *mamenka* does. I miss her even though she peck at me so much. I miss the land, too. But not *Ambrosch*. So much he is . . . so . . . *sullen*. This is a word, yes?

MRS. HARLING: A perfect word to describe the Ambrosch I met!

ÁNTONIA does a little dance of happiness at having used this word correctly. SALLY whispers in ÁNTONIA's ear.

ÁNTONIA: Mmmmm! Great idea, Silly Sally!

She tickles SALLY.

SALLY (*laughing*): And tell us a story too!

MRS. HARLING: What did she say?

ÁNTONIA: Sally would like some taffy.

JIM: I want to hear about the calf that broke its leg!

MRS. HARLING (*about the taffy*): Mmmmm.

SALLY: No—about saving the turkeys from drowning!

JIM: Caaaaalf.

SALLY: TURKEYS!

JIM: You're a turkey!

SALLY: Pbbbbttt!!

ÁNTONIA: Mrs. Harling, did you ever hear about the drifter up by the Norwegians last summer?

MRS. HARLING: I don't believe I did, Ántonia.

SALLY (*whispering*): *You're the turkey!*

MRS. HARLING: *SHHHH!*

ÁNTONIA: Oooh, it was horrible. I was threshing there—out at Ole Iverson's—

MRS. HARLING: You threw the wheat into the bin yourself?

ÁNTONIA: Oh, yes, ma'am, I did. I could shovel just as fast as the other men there, too. One day it was just awful hot when we got back to the field from dinner and we were taking it kind of easy. I was sitting against a straw-stack and after a while I see a tramp coming across the stubble. When he got close I could see his toes stuck out of his shoes and he hadn't shaved for a long while—oh, and his eyes was *awful* red and wild, like he had some kind of sickness. He comes right up to me like he know me already. He say (*imitating his voice*), "The ponds in this country is done got so low a man couldn't drownd himself in one of 'em."

I say nobody *want* to "drownd" themselves, but just to be nice I say that with no rain we'd have to pump water for the cattle.

"Oh, cattle," he say, "you'll all take care of your cattle! Ain't you got no beer here?" I told him the Norwegians didn't have none when they threshed. "My God!" he says, "so it's Norwegians now, is it? I thought this was Americy."

Then he goes up to the machine and yells out to Ole, "Hello partner, let me up there. I'll give you a hand."

I thought this man was crazy and might break the machine, but Ole was glad to get down out of the sun and jumped down right away. The tramp got on the machine and he worked for a few minutes, but then, Mrs. Harling, he waves his hand at me and *jumps head-first right into the threshing machine.*

The others gasp—"Oh my word!" "What!?!"

ÁNTONIA: Uh-huh. I begun to scream, and the men run to stop the horses, but the belt had sucked him down, and when they got it stopped, he was all beat and cut to pieces. He was wedged in so tight it was a hard job to get him out . . . And the machine ain't never worked right since.

SALLY: Was he clear dead, Tony?

ÁNTONIA: He sure was!

JIM: Why would he do that? Who was this guy?

ÁNTONIA shrugs.

MRS. HARLING: Did anyone claim him?

ÁNTONIA: Never, ma'am. They couldn't find no letters nor *nothing* on him; nothing but an old penknife . . . and a wishbone. Oh! And a poem cut out of a newspaper called, "The Old Oaken Bucket."

MRS. HARLING: Hmmm . . . mysterious.

ÁNTONIA: Ain't that strange, Mrs. Harling? I don't get why anyone would want to kill themselves in summer for.

MRS. HARLING: Beautiful time of year. Is that taffy ready to eat yet? Smells delicious.

SALLY: Yummmmmmmmmmmmmmm.

MRS. HARLING: Have I ever told you kids the story of *Rigoletto?* (*Calling off.*) Julia! How about playing from *Rigoletto?*

A selection from Rigoletto *is heard on piano.*
The children and ÁNTONIA begin playing and dancing to the music as the lights fade.

Scene 3: Dancing Makes Your Blood Flow

NARRATOR JIM: Life can't stand still, not even in the quietest of country towns and boys and girls have to grow up. That next summer was the one that changed everything.

> *The stage is transformed into a dance pavilion. This should take some time setting up. MRS. VANNI enters as the pavilion is constructed.*

MRS. VANNI (*calling out*): DANCE LESSONS! ALL AGES! SATURDAY DANCES SEVEN TO MIDNIGHT!

> *The town people begin to gather. JIM runs through the crowds to the HARLINGS' where ÁNTONIA and MRS. HARLING are preserving cherries.*

JIM: Ántonia! Mrs. Harling! They're putting up a dance tent in town!

MRS. HARLING: Who is?

JIM: Some Italians from Kansas City. They're setting up in that vacant lot by the Danish laundry—dance lessons in the afternoons and dancing *every Saturday night until midnight!*

ÁNTONIA: Oh! May I go see, Mrs. Harling? I'm through with my work . . .

MRS. HARLING: What kind of music, Jim?

JIM: I'm not sure, but I saw a harp and some violin cases.

ÁNTONIA: Oh!

MRS. HARLING: That'd be fine, Ántonia.

JIM: Come on, Tony. It looks like a merry-go-round pavilion!

> *They run through the town. The townsfolk crowd in at once. The lights suddenly switch to nighttime, an elaborate, energetic dance takes place.*

NARRATOR JIM: At last there was something to do in those long, empty summer evenings. Now the silence was broken by lighthearted sounds.

JIM (*dancing*): Why didn't we have a tent before?!?

ÁNTONIA: I love it!

> *More dancing.*

NARRATOR JIM: Country boys came in from farms eight and ten miles away, railroad men, delivery boys, the iceman . . . And all the country girls were on the floor—Ántonia and Lena and Tiny, the three Bohemian Marys, and the Danish laundry girls with their white throats and pink cheeks . . . The young professional men of town used to drop in late and risk a tiff with their sweethearts just for a waltz with the "the hired girls . . ."

ÁNTONIA: JIM!

> *She waves to him as they dance.*

NARRATOR JIM: It was at the dances that Ántonia was discovered.

> *The girls dance as the music plays. The boys retreat off to the side to talk. JIM is nearby, listening.*

SYLVESTER: I saw you dancing with the Harlings' Tony . . .

HARRY PAINE: Yeah, how about you?

SYLVESTER: Nah, it's all Thompsons' Lena for me.

HARRY PAINE: Oh-ho! Lovely Lena!

SYLVESTER: That's right.

LARRY: Yeah, Sylvester's hoping his sweetheart don't notice!

HARRY PAINE: Hey, you boys watch—I'm going to get a walk home in with Tony tonight!

SYLVESTER: Yeah, right, with your fiancée on the other arm!

LARRY: Yeah, hey, ain't you getting married *in the morning*? To your boss's *daughter*?

HARRY: Exactly—married! (*Watching ÁNTONIA.*) Look at that.

LARRY: *These hired girls could drive you up the wall.*

> *MRS. VANNI gives a signal and the harp begins playing "Home Sweet Home." The dancers stop.*

HARRY: Here we go.

MRS. VANNI: That's all for this evening, ladies and gentlemen! Remember dance lessons every day at 3 P.M.! Good night, Lena, Mary . . . Oh, *Ántonia*! Such strength and passion! You are our very best dancer!

ÁNTONIA: Thank you, Mrs. Vanni!

HARRY: Hi Tony.

ÁNTONIA: Harry.

HARRY: Walk you home?

ÁNTONIA: Oh . . . where is Elizabeth?

HARRY: Not here tonight, so.

ÁNTONIA: Oh, I don't think—

HARRY: Just a walk. I need to clear my head.

ÁNTONIA: You're getting married tomorrow, Harry.

HARRY: Come on, Ántonia. We danced so well together.

ÁNTONIA: I don't know.

HARRY: You scared? Can't two people just walk with each other regardless of who's marrying whom?

ÁNTONIA: Well, yes . . . okay.

HARRY: Good!

> *They walk. He turns and makes eyes with the boys.*

ÁNTONIA: How is Elizabeth's dress coming?

HARRY: Mrs. Vanni was right you know—you're the best one out there.

ÁNTONIA: Thank you.

HARRY: Everyone says it.

ÁNTONIA: I hope the tent never leave.

HARRY: Ha, doubt you'll see me there again. Married bank cashiers working for their father-in-law don't go out dancing too much, I guess.

ÁNTONIA: You are lucky to get married.

Harry: Yeah, maybe. If only I could quit this choking feeling in my throat.

ÁNTONIA: Oh.

HARRY: This the Harlings' place?

ÁNTONIA: Yes,

HARRY (*whistles, then*): Niiiice.

ÁNTONIA: Let's go around back . . . I don't want to wake them.

HARRY: Okay.

> *They walk in back.*

ÁNTONIA: Well, I go through here. I hope the wedding is—

> *HARRY kisses her. She pushes him away. He grabs her and pulls her back toward him, kisses her forcefully. She struggles. His hands stray down her body. They struggle. She slaps him hard.*

HARRY: Christ!

ÁNTONIA: Get out of here!

> *HARRY runs.*

MR. HARLING (*from within*): Ántonia?

ÁNTONIA (*trying to compose herself*): Mr. Harling! Yes?

MR. HARLING: Get in here, please.

> *ÁNTONIA enters.*

MR. HARLING: *This* is what I've been expecting. The girls you go to the dances with have a reputation for being free and easy, now you're no different. I won't put up with it.

ÁNTONIA: I'm sorry—

MR. HARLING: *What did you expect would happen?* This is the end of it. Tonight. It stops, short. You can quit going to these dances or you can hunt another place for work. Think it over.

> *He exits. ÁNTONIA sits.*

Scene 4: Fracture

(Morning.)

MRS. HARLING: It will be best for you, believe me. Just stop going and we'll have our fun times again.

ÁNTONIA: My own father couldn't make me stop—and Mr. Harling ain't my father!

MRS. HARLING: What you do outside of work has an effect on our family, Tony. Stop the dances and stop seeing Lena and Tiny. That's it!

ÁNTONIA: Oh, great, now I'm supposed to quit my friends?

MRS. HARLING: You go with them, you end up with Harry Paine lurking around.

ÁNTONIA: I thought Harry was fine—he used to hang around with Charley, didn't he? I guess he'll have a red face for his wedding!

> *She storms into the next room.*

ÁNTONIA: I'm not giving up my friends!

MRS. HARLING (*quiet*): This is Mr. Harling's house. It's up to you.

ÁNTONIA: Then I'll go.

> *MRS. HARLING gasps. SALLY and JIM do, too.*

MRS. HARLING: *Tony!*

SALLY: NO, PLEASE, ÁNTONIA!

ÁNTONIA: Yeah. Lena's been wanting me to get a place near her forever. I'll just take Mary Svoboda's place working for Mr. Cutter.

MRS. HARLING (*rising from her chair, severe*): Ántonia, if you go to Cutters', you cannot come back to this house again. *You know what that man is. He'll ruin you.*

ÁNTONIA (*laughing spitefully*): Ha. I'm stronger than Cutter—stronger than anyone in this town. He pays well *and* there's NO CHILDREN.

> Pause. SALLY runs from the room.

MRS. HARLING: *What has gotten into you?*

> Pause.

I thought you liked children.

ÁNTONIA: A girl's got to take her good times when she gets 'em. Maybe there won't be a tent next year—or even next week. I want to have my fling.

MRS. HARLING: You go to work for Cutter you'll have a fling you won't ever get up from.

Scene 5: After School With the Girls

(*TINY, LENA, and ÁNTONIA in gloves, high heels, feathered bonnets. The boys of town, their mouths hanging open, watch them walk past.*)

NARRATOR JIM: Ántonia went to live with the Cutters and soon seemed to care about nothing but picnics and parties and having a good time. The country girls were talked of as a menace to the social order. Sometimes I could coax the girls into the ice-cream parlor.

LENA: Larry Donovan's certainly got himself all twisted up over you, Tony.

JIM: Larry Donovan?

ÁNTONIA: Stop it—we like to dance.

TINY: Yeah, you're not the first he's danced with.

JIM: We all call him The Ladies' Man.

ÁNTONIA: Larry's nice!

TINY: Jim, I hear your grandmother's going to make a Baptist preacher out of you.

JIM: What? Where'd you hear that?

TINY: I guess you'll have to stop dancing and wear a white necktie then.

> They laugh.

LENA: Well, you'll have to hurry up, Jim. I want you to be the preacher for my wedding. You can for all of us. Then you can baptize the babies.

TINY: Baptists don't believe in baptizing babies, do they, Jim?

JIM: I don't know! And I don't care! I'm not going to be a preacher!

TINY: That's too bad . . . You'd be a good one. Or! *Maybe* you could be a professor. Didn't you used to teach Tony?

JIM: Yeah . . .

ÁNTONIA: No, no, no, my heart's set on Jim being a doctor. You'd be good with sick people, Jim. Your grandmother trained you up so nice.

LENA: *She sure did.*

JIM: I'm gonna be whatever I feel like—I don't care what anyone in town says. Maybe I'll grow up and be a right devil of a fellow like Larry!

TINY: Rest easy, Mr. Devil, everyone in town already thinks you're a sly one.

JIM: Jeez, what is this?

ÁNTONIA: Oh, yeah, we hear everyone say, "How come he always with the hired girls? How come he never with girls his own age?"

JIM: Which ones—Owl Club girls? Bankers' daughters? Buncha sleepwalkers. UGH!

LENA: You like us *dangerous* girls too much.

JIM: Can you blame me?

Scene 6: Jim the Sneak

NARRATOR JIM: I refused to join the Owl Club for dances, and every Saturday night after the old people had gone to bed I sneaked out to go dancing at the Firemen's hall.

> *JIM sneaks off to the dance at the Firemen's hall. We see a dance number. Eventually, dancers freeze except JIM and ÁNTONIA. They dance.*

JIM: Where's Larry tonight?

ÁNTONIA: Oh, out on the rails somewhere . . . He'll be back next week.

JIM: May I walk you home . . . later?

> *She nods, smiles. The intensity of the dance and their connection while they dance strengthens.*

JIM: You look really—

> *The dancers unfreeze and rejoin the music. The dance finishes. JIM and ÁNTONIA walk home together. Stage grows quiet in the darkness of the night.*

JIM: You dance differently from Lena.

ÁNTONIA: How?

JIM: Just different. She's more languorous. Indolent even.

ÁNTONIA: I don't know these words, Professor.

JIM (smiles): Sort of sleepy, or lazy. Like she's dreaming or coming in with the tide. It's nice.

> They walk.

JIM: Look at all these houses. Everyone asleep. Ugh.

ÁNTONIA: Here we are.

JIM: What's with all the trees in front of the house?

ÁNTONIA: Mrs. Cutter say she want privacy.

JIM: Yeesh. This place is creepier than Pavel's cabin.

ÁNTONIA: No, Pavel's was much nicer!

> They laugh.

JIM: Hey. Um.

ÁNTONIA: Yes . . . ?

JIM: We've been friends a long time.

ÁNTONIA: My longest friend!

JIM: So, I think you should kiss me good night.

> Pause.

ÁNTONIA: Okay. I could do that.

> JIM kisses her deeply. She hesitates, then kisses him back hard. They break.

ÁNTONIA (whispering): Jim! You know you ain't right to kiss me like that!

JIM: Why not?

> He moves to kiss her again.

ÁNTONIA: No! Jim! I'll tell your grandmother on you!

JIM: Lena lets me kiss her—

ÁNTONIA: She what?

JIM: And I like you *more*.

ÁNTONIA: You've been kissing Lena?

JIM: Uh-huh.

ÁNTONIA: If she's up to her nonsense with you, I'll scratch her eyes out!

JIM: She likes me.

ÁNTONIA: Come on . . .

JIM: Did you hear what I said?

> *Pause.*

ÁNTONIA: Look, don't be a fool like the other boys round here. Just fools who going to sit at home all their life telling stories. Ugh! You go away to school, see oceans and the world.

JIM: Away from you—

ÁNTONIA: *Yes.* I want you to do big things. *I'm proud of you.*

JIM: You're the only one I care about.

ÁNTONIA: Tsk.

JIM: I guess I'm just a little kid to you still.

ÁNTONIA: Well, yeah. But, a kid I like a lot!

> *She laughs and gives him a jab. JIM shakes his head.*

ÁNTONIA: Listen, if I see you with Lena, I'm gonna tell your grandmother. Stay away from her!

JIM: *I get it.* What about Larry?

> *She doesn't answer. They linger.*

ÁNTONIA: Okay . . . Mr. Cutter don't like me to bring boys nearby . . . He always watch for me after the dances.

JIM: He waits for you?

> *A shadow.*

ÁNTONIA: Oh, there he is!

> *She hugs him again.*

JIM: Good night . . .

> *She exits into her house. JIM walks home.*

JIM (*shouting at the houses*): I KNOW WHO THE REAL WOMEN ARE, YOU MICE! AND I'M NOT AFRAID OF THEM EITHER!

> *A dog barks. JIM realizes what he's done and runs.*

NARRATOR JIM: That night I dreamed a dream I'd had many times. It was always the same. I was in a harvest-field full of shocks, and I was lying against one of them. Lena came across the stubble barefoot, in a short skirt, with a curved reaping hook in her hand, and she was flushed like the dawn. She sat down beside me, and with a soft sigh said . . . "Now they are all gone, and I can kiss you as much as I like."

I used to wish I could have this dream about Ántonia. But I never did.

SCENE 7: MRS. HARLING LISTENS

(The Harlings' front porch.)

MRS. HARLING: What's eating you, Jim?

JIM: Grandmother asked me to stop going to the dances.

MRS. HARLING: I wondered when she'd catch you.

JIM: You knew?

> *She gives him a look.*

JIM: I don't understand what the problem is! It's just dancing!

MRS. HARLING: I'm as broad-minded as a mother can be, but you know I was hurt by Tony.

JIM: I know.

MRS. HARLING: I loved her like I do Julia and Sally.

JIM: I know, but she's—.

MRS. HARLING: And I've heard the way you defend her, but it's hard for me to agree with you. Your grandparents are worried about you. They're afraid—

JIM: I don't know why.

MRS. HARLING: They can't understand why you like to be with Tony and Lena and Tiny instead of town girls your own age.

JIM: Ha. I've danced with those girls. They don't move! It's like their muscles are asking one thing—not to be disturbed!

> *He imitates them—goes slack. MRS. HARLING laughs at this, nods.*

JIM: I bet *you* understand why I like Tony and the girls.

MRS. HARLING: Oh, I think I do! I have eyes.

JIM: It's more than that.

MRS. HARLING: I know. You knew them in the country, you understand them. But, your grandparents would like you to join in with your own *set* and you need to respect that.

JIM: What does that mean, *"my own set"*? I should grow up and marry some nice, dull, town girl? Great, I'll live in some flimsy little Black Hawk house where I and my jealous wife can admire all the immaculate chairs we own that, oh, by the way, MUST NOT BE SAT UPON, and our hand-painted china that, remember! MUST NOT BE USED! Who cares if some of the girls like to dance and laugh every now and then? Every one of them still sends money back to her family on the farm—they're all *working*. And did you know Lena's grandfather was a clergyman back in Norway? And there isn't a man in this town who has the intelligence and cultivation that Ántonia's dad had! Oh, but who cares! They're all foreigners and foreigners are stupid and can't speak English. "You'll probably catch some disease from them." UGH!

MRS. HARLING: My!

JIM: Sorry.

MRS. HARLING: You do like to take sides, don't you? That will serve you well. If you're on the right side.

JIM: If you were a boy, you wouldn't join the Owl Club—you'd be just like me.

MRS. HARLING: Hm. Maybe. But, I think I know the country girls better than you. You're forgetting I was one once. You always put a kind of glamour over them. You're a romantic. Tell me, are you still planning on taking college exams?

JIM: Yes. My commencement oration's next week.

MRS. HARLING: I'd like to hear it.

JIM: I'd love for you to be there.

MRS. HARLING: I want to see how serious you can be.

SCENE 8: CUTTER CIRCLES

NARRATOR JIM: The day after commencement I moved my books and desk upstairs, to an empty room and I fell to studying in earnest.

>JIM paces his attic room in sunlight, attempts to memorize passages from the Aeneid.

JIM: *Agnosco veteris vestigias flamas* . . . I feel once the old scars of the—
Agnosco veteris vestigias flamas . . . I feel once more the *scars* of the old flame.
Agnosco veteris vestigias flamas—

GRANDMOTHER (*from downstairs*): Well, look who it is!

>JIM exits downstairs to the kitchen.

NARRATOR JIM: One morning I came down to find Ántonia in our kitchen.

GRANDMOTHER: Why, Ántonia: you look like a raccoon.

ÁNTONIA (*to Grandma*): Yes, I couldn't . . . sleep last night.

GRANDMOTHER: What's the trouble?

ÁNTONIA: Mr. Cutter. He go away with Mrs. Cutter to Omaha.

GRANDMOTHER: Together? That's odd.

ÁNTONIA: She like to keep a watch on him.

GRANDMOTHER: Those two . . .

    Pause.

ÁNTONIA: Before he go he . . . make me feel . . . I don't know what it is. First he put all his silver in a basket. He place a box of papers he say are valuable under my bed. Then he make me promise I won't sleep away from the house while he leave. I say I don't want to watch his things.

GRANDMOTHER: Oh, dear.

ÁNTONIA: He does have many belongings he have to protect, but . . . he keep staring at me before he go and he stand so close saying over and over, "Stay right in your bed." He is scare me. I'm silly.

GRANDMOTHER: I don't think you should stay there. You're not silly. Sleep here.

ÁNTONIA: But, he say—

GRANDMOTHER: No, you're right: *Someone* should stay there. You did give your word.

    Thinks it over. They both look at JIM.

JIM: What?

GRANDMOTHER: Maybe you could do it.

JIM: Do what?

GRANDMOTHER: Take care of Cutter's silver and notes while Ántonia sleeps here.

ÁNTONIA: Yes! That could— Jim, would you do it?

JIM: Eh, I don't know . . .

ÁNTONIA: You can sleep in my bed.

JIM: I like my room. My books are here.

GRANDMOTHER: I'd feel much safer knowing Ántonia was here with us, son.

ÁNTONIA: It's a real cool room and the bed's right near the window . . . Only, last night I was afraid to open it.

> *Pause.*

Please?

JIM: Alright, I'll do it.

> *She kisses his cheek.*

ÁNTONIA: Thank you!

GRANDMOTHER: I'll let Grandfather know.

> *GRANDMOTHER exits, ÁNTONIA makes to exit, stops.*

ÁNTONIA: Oh, hey! Tiny, me and Lena are going to the river Sunday. Anna says the elder's all in bloom now.

JIM: I bet it's bursting.

ÁNTONIA: Come with us! We'll take a nice lunch and we can picnic. Just us; nobody else.

> *Pause.*

JIM: I'll meet you there.

Scene 9: Picnic

NARRATOR JIM: I slept well at the Cutters' place. On Sunday morning, I left early to visit the river. It was my only holiday that summer.

> *JIM swims. The stage transforms to become the river with its bluffs and trees and flowers. The girls enter.*

JIM: HELLO! Down here!

> *The girls stop their horse and they peer down at JIM below. JIM waves.*

JIM: How pretty you look!

LENA and ÁNTONIA: So do you!

> *They laugh.*
> *JIM dresses. JIM and NARRATOR JIM watch the girls as they begin to fan themselves and stand on the edge of the ravine.*
> *The girls set off with their baskets in search of the elder.*

JIM (*calling*): I'll catch up with you!

> *They wave, sing together as they walk.*

NARRATOR JIM: I followed a cattle path through the thick underbrush until I came to a slope where I saw Ántonia seated alone under the luxuriant, pagoda-like elders.

ÁNTONIA is crying. JIM sidles up close to her.

JIM: What's the matter?

ÁNTONIA: I am *velmi* homesick.

JIM: Bohemia?

ÁNTONIA (*nodding*): We have this flower very much at home. My papa had a green bench and a table under a bush like this in our yard . . .

JIM is silent.

ÁNTONIA: In summer he sit with his friend and they talk. It was such beautiful talk, not like you hear in this country at all.

JIM: What about?

ÁNTONIA: Music and God and back when they were boys.

JIM: I think he's back there now.

ÁNTONIA: You do?

He nods. Pause.

JIM: Some day I am going to Bohemia. I want to see your town. Do you remember it?

ÁNTONIA: If I was put down there in the middle of the night, I could find my way all over that little town. My feet remember all the little paths through the woods. I ain't never forgot my own country.

JIM: We should go there.

ÁNTONIA smiles at him.

LENA (*entering above them, out of breath*): You lazy things! All this elder and us so hot in the sun and you're just laying there together. Get up here!

JIM runs up the bank to LENA. He is trailed by ÁNTONIA.

ÁNTONIA: Look! There's Ole Iverson's land . . .

TINY: Jim, you see my father's land?

JIM: Where?

TINY: Just over the second valley . . .

JIM: Oh, I see it.

TINY: Seventy acres wheat this year and a hundred twenty corn. He's doing good!

LENA: Can you imagine being a mother and coming to this country like ours did?

TINY: My grandmother's so feeble she thinks she's at home in Norway! She keeps asking mother to take her down to the waterside for fish . . .

ÁNTONIA: Poor thing!

LENA: I'm going to get my mother out of that old sod house. The men will never do it . . . Maybe I'll marry a rich gambler . . .

ÁNTONIA: Oh, Lena . . .

LENA (*A change of subject*): Mercy, it's hot! (*She stretches out and leans against a tree.*) Come here, Jim. You never got the sand out of your hair.

> JIM *sits in between her legs, his back to her.* LENA *begins slowly drawing her fingers through his hair.*

ÁNTONIA (*sharp*): Ach, you'll never get it out like that . . .

> *She reaches over and roughly brushes the sand out of* JIM's *hair, boxes him on the ear and pushes him away.*

JIM: Gee, Ántonia . . .

ÁNTONIA (*kicking* LENA'S *high-heeled shoes*): Lena, you oughtn't wear such shoes. They're too small for your feet.

LENA: My shoes are perfect.

> (*Silence.* LENA *begins to hum a tune, one they all know, as they look out over the bluffs.* TINY *joins her quietly, also humming. Then* ÁNTONIA *starts to sing the tune louder. Their voices grow together and finally* JIM *joins them.*)

LENA: Look!

> *They stand.*

NARRATOR JIM: The sun was going down in a limpid, gold-washed sky. Just as the lower edge of the red disk rested against the horizon, a great black figure suddenly appeared on the face of the sun.

> *The group sees the image,*

JIM: What is that?

NARRATOR JIM: On some upland farm, a plough had been left in the field. The sun was sinking behind it. Magnified across the distance by the horizontal light, it stood out black against the molten red.

ÁNTONIA (*whispering*): My God.

> ÁNTONIA *holds* JIM's *hand.*

NARRATOR JIM: A picture writing on the sun.

Scene 10: Wick Cutter

(That night. JIM is sleeping. The sound of a door opening.)

JIM (*hopeful*): Ántonia?

> *He listens. Goes back to sleep. A shadow creeps into the room. It approaches JIM slowly, sits on the edge of the bed. Touches JIM's hip and caresses it. Leans down, then lays on top of JIM, his hand reaching between JIM's legs. JIM grabs CUTTER's face and screams. CUTTER yells, clutches JIM's throat. They struggle.*

CUTTER: What the hell? So, this is what she's up to while I'm away, eh? A little action under the sheets?

> *CUTTER begins beating him mercilessly in the face.*

CUTTER: WHERE ARE YOU? COME OUT NOW, YOU LITTLE—YOU *HUSSY*! I KNOW YOUR TRICKS! (*Punches JIM again*) WHERE IS SHE?!? JUST WAIT UNTIL I GET AT YOU, HUSSY, I'M GOING TO SPLIT YOU WIDE OPEN!

> *He begins to choke JIM. JIM gets hold of one of CUTTER's fingers and bends it far back. CUTTER yowls, releases JIM. JIM runs out. He runs home. He explodes through the front door and collapses on the floor of the parlor. GRANDMOTHER, awakened by the commotion, finds JIM, gives a cry of fright.*

GRANDMOTHER: Jim! Oh, my Lord—*What happened?*

> *JIM moans.*

GRANDMOTHER: Where are you hurt? Oh, dear Jesus . . . there's blood all over. There's blood— Uh . . . um . . . okay, let's get you up, son, careful.

> *She helps him to sitting up, he sucks in a breath, his ribs possibly broken as well as his nose and face. She kneels down before him, examines him.*

GRANDMOTHER: Oh, Lord, we need the doctor.

JIM: NO!

GRANDMOTHER: *Jim.* You've got—oh Lord your eye is cut —your nose and—

JIM: No, no doctor. *Please*, Grandmother.

GRANDMOTHER: We need him at once—

JIM: I beg you, please, don't tell anyone, I can handle it, *please*—

GRANDMOTHER: Jim, what has gotten into you?

JIM: *Please*—

> *A knock at the door. It is ÁNTONIA.*

ÁNTONIA: Jim? Mrs. Burden?

> *GRANDMOTHER stands to get the door.*

JIM: NO!

ÁNTONIA (*through closed door*): What's happening? Jim, are you alright? What's going on?

GRANDMOTHER: It's alright, Ántonia, Jim is—

JIM: *Don't say anything please.*

GRANDMOTHER: He's just . . . a little banged up.

ÁNTONIA: *What?* What happened?

GRANDMOTHER: It's alright.

ÁNTONIA: Let me in!

JIM: NO!

ÁNTONIA: Please let me in! Jim! *What's going on?*

JIM (*at ÁNTONIA*): GET OUT OF HERE!

ÁNTONIA: *Jim—*

JIM: GO!!! I NEVER WANT TO SEE YOU AGAIN!!!

    Blackout.

ACT III
YOUNG ADULTHOOD

SCENE 1: GASTON AND JIM

(JIM sitting at a desk studying. A knock on the door. He answers it. GASTON CLERIC.)

GASTON: Oh, Lincoln. Lincoln, Lincoln, Lincoln, Lincoln—

JIM: Good morning, Professor Cleric.

GASTON: Lincoln, Lincoln, Lincoln, Lincoln, Lincoln—I told you to call me Gaston—Lincoln, Lincoln, Lincoln, Lincoln, *Lincoln . . . NEBRASKA!!!*

JIM: Home Sweet Home.

GASTON: You staying for the summer? *I've* been instructed to cancel my return to the east for it might further "enfeeble" me.

JIM: *Enfeeble?*

GASTON: That's what they said—*enfeeble.* And I had to say, Look, doctor, could you be more precise? I'm a professor of Latin—I trade in words—so, please, tell me, do you mean "enfeeble" as in going to Boston will somehow "further weaken my health" or "enfeeble" as in two months on the coast will "diminish my character" because if it's the latter I would argue that a *return* to New England is *precisely* what the doctor should be ordering. I dare say if one sign of a worldly man is his *worldliness,* as in, *has spent time in the world,* then *more* time in Lincoln, Nebraska, will be an exacerbating *cause* of a rapid diminishment in character, and therefore—character, wit, and culture being the nutrients they are—*more* time in *Lincoln, Nebraska,* will see my expiry *through.*

He has a short coughing fit.

JIM: I like Lincoln.

GASTON: I know, I know, you're a Nebraska boy—he of the seed prices and crop yields, lover of corn and golden-hued wheat—but, Jim, it's dead here.

JIM: It's a small town, but compared to Black Hawk—

GASTON: Small town! You know what an example of a small town is to me? Chicago. Chicago is a small town, this is the absolute barren end of the Earth.

JIM: You've seen Paris.

GASTON: I've lived in Rome! The source of western thought!

JIM: You know what, Gaston? *You're* like the Romans. You bring culture to the heathens in the untamed wild west. Just without the sword on your belt.

GASTON: Ah, yes, good, *perfect*: I'll think of it that way. That'll sustain me. (*At the window*) HEY, *CORN*! WANT TO HEAR ABOUT VIRGIL'S *GEORGICS*? OR HOW ABOUT THE TRAGIC THEATRE AT POMPEII?! NO? (*Waits for an answer.*) It's just staring at me.

JIM (*laughing*): I think you've got its attention!

GASTON (*looking out the window*): How can you live way out here? At least I live in the *center* of Lincoln where there are *people*.

JIM: I like the prairie. It keeps my mind open. Plus it reminds me of home. Best of both worlds.

GASTON: Yeah, right.

> GASTON *gets ready to go.*

Anyway, you're staying, right?

JIM: For the summer? Yeah.

GASTON: Good. You can revive me if I choke to death on the dust.

JIM: Sure thing.

GASTON (*exiting*): We still going to the theater tomorrow?

JIM: Definitely.

GASTON: Good. BACK TO YOUR VIRGIL, COWBOY!

JIM (*laughing*): See you.

> GASTON *raises his hand as he exits.*

Scene 2: Gaston and Jim and Virgil

(*JIM sitting at a desk studying. A knock on the door. He answers it. GASTON CLERIC.*)

GASTON: I've been walking.

JIM: Come in.

GASTON: You have any of that Benedictine?

JIM: Right here.

GASTON: Good man. Jesus, I feel shaky.

> *JIM gets GASTON a drink. GASTON coughs violently.*

JIM: Sounds kind of rough.

GASTON: *Optima dies . . . prima fugit.* "The best days are the first to flee." I can't shake that line, Burden. No matter how many times I read it.

JIM: Me neither.

GASTON: *Primus ego in patriam mecum . . . deducam Musas—*

JIM: "For I shall be the first, if I live, to bring the Muse into my country."

GASTON: That *if* in "*if* I live . . ."

> *Pause.*

When Virgil was dying at Brindisi, he must have remembered that passage. Remember, this was after he had faced the bitter fact that he would leave the *Aeneid* unfinished, and after he had decreed that that great canvas—*his* canvas—should be burned rather than survive him unperfected. His mind must have gone back to the perfect utterances of his *Georgics—*

JIM: His pen fitted to the matter as the plough is to the furrow.

GASTON:—Yes—*wow,* Burden, ever considered writing poetry?—He must have gone back to the perfect utterances of his *Georgics* and he must have said to himself, with the thankfulness of a good man, "I was the first to bring the Muse into my country."

> *Silence, punctuated by GASTON's wracking coughs.*

SCENE 3: LENA AND JIM

(JIM sitting at a desk studying. A knock on the door. He answers it. LENA LINGARD.)

LENA: Hi, Jim.

> *Pause.*

You don't know me.

JIM: Lena?

> *Pause.*

Hello! Um. HELLO!

LENA (*strolling into room*): Nice room.

JIM: It is—I am. I—Yes. Um, *Lena*, how did you—*What are you doing here?*

LENA: I live here.

JIM: Where?

LENA: In Lincoln. Just like you, mister.

JIM: You do?!?

LENA: I own a dressmaking shop.

JIM: You—?!? Where is it?

LENA: In the Raleigh Block over on O Street. I've made a real good start.

JIM: That's . . . wonderful. But, when did you move?

LENA: I've been here since winter.

JIM: *What?*

LENA: Didn't your grandmother write you? I thought about stopping by, but we've all heard what a studious young man you are. And . . . I didn't know if you'd be happy to see me. Have I changed much?

JIM: You're prettier, if that's possible.

LENA: You like my new suit? I have to dress pretty well in my business.

JIM: Dressmaker.

LENA: This summer I'll be able to pay for that new house for Mother I've always talked about. I have it all planned.

JIM: Wow, Lena. You must feel really proud of yourself. I hope you do. Look at me: I've never earned a dollar. Who knows if I ever will!

LENA: Ha. That's not how Tony sees it. She says you'll be richer than Mr. Harling one day. She's always bragging about you, you know.

JIM: *How is Tony?*

LENA: I knew you'd want to hear about her.

JIM: Of course.

LENA: Of course.

> *Pause.*

LENA: She's fine. Working for Mrs. Gardener now at the hotel. She's made it up with Mrs. Harling, too.

JIM: Oh, good. I always felt bad about that situation. Mrs. Harling and Tony seemed so alike to me. Is she still going with Larry?

LENA: Yes! Worse than ever. They're engaged.

JIM: *What*?

LENA: Tony talks about him like he was president of the railroad. Everyone laughs, but she won't hear a word against him.

JIM: *God.* Oh, yes, Larry the train-crew aristocrat! So afraid that someone might ask him to put up a car-window, and if requested to perform such a *menial service*, silently points to the button that calls the porter. Gah, I can't stand that guy! I can't *believe* Ántonia fell for it!

LENA: Some of us could tell her some other things about Larry, but it wouldn't do any good. She'll always believe him.

JIM: Ugh—engaged?!? Ántonia, no!

LENA: I knew you'd hate it. (*Leans in close to look at his books.*) What are you studying? So that's Latin, is it?

JIM: Yes.

LENA: Hm. Looks hard.

> *Pause.*

> Well, it's been awful good to see you.

JIM: You don't have to go, do you? We've hardly talked.

LENA: I'm a busy woman, Jim.

JIM: Can I come visit you?

LENA: Would you like to? I'd love that. I'm almost never busy after six o'clock. I know you go to the theatre. I've seen you there.

JIM: And you didn't say hello?

LENA: Maybe we could go to a play together. I can't stay at home if there's a good one in town. Have you seen the posters for *Camille?*

JIM: Yes, let's!

LENA: Come and see me next time you're lonesome. But maybe you have all the friends you want.

> *Whispers in his ear, leaning in close.*

> *Have you?*

> *LENA exits. JIM stands watching her. He turns back to his room.*

Scene 4: Courtship

NARRATOR JIM: For months after that I met Lena downtown after my morning classes. We spent afternoons walking, evenings out at the theater, long Sunday breakfasts. Lena was never so pretty as in the morning.

> (JIM and LENA having their Sunday coffee, very comfortable with each other. They burst out laughing, Jim is performing for her, pretending to act in Camille.)

JIM (*to the audience, for LENA'S benefit*): "Look, all of you, I owe this woman nothing!"

LENA/JIM: "NOTHING!"

JIM: And then he flung the bank notes at the half-swooning Marguerite—OH!

LENA: None of the plays we'll ever see will be half as gorgeous as *Camille*.

JIM: Probably not.

> He sits, holds her hand, she squeezes it. They sit close. Violin music is heard in the next room.

JIM: Who's playing?

LENA: That's Ordinsky, my Polish violinist neighbor. Always sending me the most beautiful music from across the hall . . . I think he and my old landlord are in love with me.

JIM: The *Colonel*?

LENA: Yes . . .

> They listen to the music.

JIM: Want to dance?

LENA: Why sure.

> They dance.

JIM: Remember the Vannis' tent?

> She smiles. They keep dancing slowly. The violin stops abruptly. They keep dancing close. ORDINSKY cuts in with a different tune, something peppy and fast. JIM and LENA start laughing. JIM does a funny dance. They are loud. The violin music stops.

ORDINSKY (*off, pounding on the wall; "Quit the ruckus!"*): Przestańcie robić ten hałas!

> JIM and LENA gasp and laugh some more, trying to keep it down. LENA kisses JIM.

JIM: What's it like having three men in love with you?

SCENE 5: GASTON'S EXIT

NARRATOR JIM: Lena had broken my serious mood. I wasn't interested in my classes. I was drifting. Before the first of June, Gaston confronted me.

GASTON: We're moving, Burden.

JIM: Where we going?

GASTON: East. Boston. I've been offered an instructorship at Harvard.

JIM: Gaston!

GASTON: Yes . . .

JIM: You'll be home!

GASTON: Yes, the city that beckons . . . and I can finally answer. Not a day too soon, I might add. My health be damned.

JIM: Harvard!

GASTON: Yes, and this fall you should follow me there.

JIM: But how?

GASTON: I'll vouch for you. You need this.

JIM: That's awfully kind of you, Gaston, but—

GASTON: Look, you're done here. You need to either quit school and go to work, or change colleges and begin again. You're too far gone—you won't recover while you're playing about with this hot Norwegian.

JIM: You've met Lena?

GASTON: No, but I know all about her. How could I not? I see you with her at the theatre almost every weekend. She's pretty, Burden. I'll say. And perfectly irresponsible, from what I can tell. Take up with her for good and get a job, or begin again with me in Boston. There are no other choices, if you're to make something of yourself.

JIM: I might love her.

GASTON: You need to decide. Girls like that do not make wives. I'll write your grandfather to recommend your transfer. Just let me know.

SCENE 6: JIM SAYS GOODBYE

(*LENA sitting at a table, working. A knock on the door. She answers it. JIM BURDEN.*)

LENA: Hello, stranger.

> JIM smiles, lingers.

LENA: Well, are you going to make a decision? Come in, mister.

JIM: Ha. Okay.

> *JIM paces.*

LENA: Listen to this: I just got word that Tiny—you remember Tiny?—is running a lodging house for *sailors* up in *Seattle*. Word has it she's doing *very well* for herself.

JIM: Is that right? Sounds wild. I wonder how she can keep it up?

LENA: Tiny will find a way. She was always smarter than she let on.

> *Pause.*

JIM: I bet that old landlord of yours will be proposing to you one of these days, Lena.

LENA: He already has, about a hundred times!

JIM: And what do you tell him?

LENA: I tell him "no!"

JIM: Good. I mean—I hope you don't marry some old guy; even a rich one.

LENA: I'm not going to marry anybody, Jim. I've told you that.

JIM: Yeah, I know. That's what girls always *say*, but I know better. Every beautiful girl like you marries.

LENA: Not me.

JIM: I don't believe you.

LENA: It's true.

JIM: But why not?

LENA (*laughing*): Well, mainly because I don't want a husband. Oh, men are alright for friends, but as soon as you marry them they turn into cranky old fathers, even the wild ones. They begin to tell you what's sensible, what's foolish, how the world should work, and they're all so lost up inside their heads dreaming of other times they stop listening. *And* they always want a girl to stick at home and take care of everything for them while they pretend they're the ones getting things done. I prefer to be foolish when I feel like it, go out when I want, and be accountable to nobody.

JIM: That sounds lonesome to me. You'll get tired of it, I'm sure. You'll want a family. I know it.

LENA: HA! I *like* to be lonesome. Did you know when I went to work for Mrs. Thomas I'd never slept a single night in my life when there weren't three others in the bed with me? I never had a *minute* to myself except when I was off with *cattle*. I could never get the smell off me. The few underclothes I had I kept in a crackerbox to try and keep them fresh smelling. Ugh. That was no life for me! *Marriage. Babies.* To me, a home is a place where there are always too many children, a cross man sulking in the corner and work piling up around a sick woman. No thank you! I've had plenty of that life to last me.

JIM: It's not all like that.

LENA: What's on your mind, Jim? Are you afraid I'll want you to marry me someday?

JIM: No! Well—yes. I'm. I'm going away, Lena. To Boston. I'm—going to study at Harvard. Gaston got a new job teaching there and he invited me and I, well, I accepted.

> *Pause.*

LENA: Why do you want to go away? Haven't I been good to you?

JIM: *Yes.* I've loved being with you, Lena. I don't think about much else.

LENA: Then why are you leaving?

JIM: That's just it—when I'm with you I *can't* think of anything else.

LENA: And that's so bad?

JIM: I'm supposed to be in school. If I stay here I'll never settle down and really grind it. You know?

LENA: Sure. Sure.

> *JIM sits down next to her. They stare at the floor. She reaches for his hand.*

LENA: I never should have started this, huh?

JIM: I'm glad you did.

LENA: I couldn't really help it. I guess I've always been a little foolish about you. I don't know why. Even when you were a kid. I let you alone for a while, though, didn't I?

JIM: You did. Some.

LENA: You aren't sorry I came to see you?

JIM: Of course not.

> *She kisses him. Long, soft, slow.*

LENA (*nudges him playfully, laughing instead of crying*): You were such a funny kid!

> *She kisses him again. And again. Pushes him away. Appearing confident, over it.*

LENA: Okay, go, Jim Burden. Go be a scholar. Or write poetry—or a play!

JIM: The next *Camille?*

LENA: Hm. Yes. Just don't make the Norwegian girl die in the end. I'm going to live a long time.

>*He kisses her.*

JIM: Goodbye, Lena.

LENA: You're going, but you haven't gone yet, have you?

>*They kiss deeply and don't stop. Lights.*

Scene 7: Mrs. Harling

(MRS. HARLING tightly lit. She talks to the audience as if we were JIM.)

MRS. HARLING: I'm glad you've come back. Some of us here have wanted to see you for a long time.

>*Pause.*

It's a big change to hear everyone calling her "Poor Ántonia," you're right. Though, she's been called that for quite some time now.

She was here almost every day to do her sewing that summer before she married. I never saw a girl work harder to go to housekeeping right and well-prepared. And always singing her Bohemian songs, like she was the happiest thing in the world.

The first thing that troubled her was when Larry wrote that his train run had been changed, and they would have to live in Denver. "I'm a country girl," she said, "I doubt if I'll be able to manage so well for him in a city." She cheered up, though, and the day soon came for her to leave.

Ambrosch did the right thing by her before she left for Denver. He gave her three hundred dollars in wages for all those years he hired her out. Just like he said he would.

Well, we had a letter saying she got to Denver safe, and Larry was there to meet her. They were to be married in a few days. The next week Mrs. Shimerda got a postal card, saying she was "well and happy." After that we heard nothing. Months went by.

One night one of the farmhands said that he'd passed a livery team from town, driving fast on the west road. In the back seat there was a woman all bundled up; he thought it was Ántonia Shimerda, or Ántonia *Donovan*, as her name ought to be.

The next morning I drove out to the Shimerdas' place. The lines outside were full of washing and I saw a sight that made my heart sink—all those underclothes we'd sewed the summer before, out there swinging in the wind. When I went in, Ántonia was standing over the tubs.

"I'm not married," she says to me very quiet, "and I ought to be. He's run away. I don't know if he ever meant to marry me."

Turns out, Larry didn't have any job when she got there. He'd been fired. He lived with Ántonia till all her money gave out. One night, he just didn't come back.

Jimmy, I sat right down on that bank beside her and I cried. I was just about heart-broke. My Ántonia, that had so much good in her, come home disgraced. And Lena Lingard, that was always a bad one, say what you will, had turned out so well, and was coming home here every summer in her silks and satins, and doing so much for her mother.

All that spring and summer Tony did the work of a man on the farm. She was quiet and steady. Folks respected her industry and tried to treat her as if nothing had happened, but she was crushed.

When the winter began Ántonia started wearing a man's long overcoat and boots. One night in December, she got her cattle home, turned them into the corral, went into the house, into her room behind the kitchen, and shut the door. There she bore her child.

We were just sitting down to supper when Mrs. Shimerda came running down the basement stairs, out of breath and screeching: "Baby come, baby come! Ambrosch much like devil!"

We got over there as quick as humanly possible. I went right in to help Ántonia. After I'd dressed the baby, I took it out to show Ambrosch. He was muttering behind the stove. "You'd better put it out in the rain-barrel," he says.

Her tone becomes furious.

"Now see here, Ambrosch," I said, "there's a law in this land, don't forget that. I stand here as witness that this baby has come into the world sound and strong, and I intend to keep an eye on what befalls it! I'm watching you!" I pride myself I cowed him.

Ántonia's got on fine. She loved that baby from the first night as dearly as if she'd had a ring on her finger, and was *never* ashamed of it. She's a year and eight months old now, and no baby was ever better cared-for. Ántonia is a natural-born mother. I wish she could marry and raise a family, but I don't know as there's much chance now.

You should go to visit her, Jim. I'm sure she'd love to see you.

SCENE 8: JIM AND ÁNTONIA

(ÁNTONIA working alone. She is thin, wan-looking, but still energetic. JIM approaches. A moment or two before she notices him.)

ÁNTONIA: I thought you'd come.

JIM: I wanted to.

> *Pause.*

ÁNTONIA: I heard you were at the Harlings'.

JIM: Yes.

ÁNTONIA: I've been looking for you all day. I knew you'd come.

> *She holds out her hand to him, as she did when she was a girl. He takes it and they walk.*

JIM: I'm . . . leaving again soon. To go back east.

> *Pause.*

ÁNTONIA: Where east?

JIM: Boston. At Harvard, where I've been going. I'm going to study the law now.

ÁNTONIA: Study the law?

JIM: To become a lawyer.

ÁNTONIA: Jim the lawyer?

JIM: I know . . .

ÁNTONIA: But, what about poems and theater? Lena said—

JIM: I'm 20 years old now.

ÁNTONIA: I'm 24.

> *Pause.*

JIM: I had this great teacher in Lincoln named Gaston Cleric. He's the reason I ended up out in Boston the last two years—God, it's been so long since we talked!—

ÁNTONIA: *So* long!

JIM: Anyway, he died last winter. Pneumonia.

ÁNTONIA: I'm sorry.

JIM: I really believe he missed being a great poet. I mean, he could have been, but, he . . . squandered too much feeling . . . in the heat of talk. He was *always* telling us stories and these just brilliant insights into poetry and life when he should have been writing it all down!

ÁNTONIA: You should write it down for him.

JIM: Hm. Maybe I will. When he died, I realized I can't be a scholar. I'd get lost in that life, shut off from everyone, I'd be always yearning for *you* and everything *here*.

> *Pause.*

Then one of my mother's relatives contacted me. Said I could work in his law office in New York when I'm done. And that sort of sealed the deal. New York! I can't imagine.

ÁNTONIA: Of course, it means you're going away for good.

JIM: No . . .

ÁNTONIA: Do you like living in a city?

JIM: I've learned to love it in many ways.

ÁNTONIA: I'd always be miserable. I'd die of lonesomeness. I like to be where I
know every stack and tree, and where all the ground is friendly. I want to live
and die here. I'm going to raise my girl here.

JIM: She's beautiful.

ÁNTONIA: You met?

JIM: Back at the house.

ÁNTONIA: She is my heart walking around on little legs.

JIM: She's lucky to have you.

ÁNTONIA: I can't wait until she's old enough to tell her about all the things we
used to do. And I want to tell her about my papa.

JIM: Tony.

ÁNTONIA: I feel him here. Same with you. It's why I'll never be lonesome.

JIM: Tony.

ÁNTONIA: Yes?

JIM: I think about you all the time. More than anyone else. You really are a part of me.

> *Pause.*

ÁNTONIA: How can you say that when you know so many people and after I've
. . . disappointed you? I am nothing.

JIM: There's no one else who means more.

> *Pause.*

ÁNTONIA: I'm so glad we had each other when we were little.

JIM: Me too.

NARRATOR JIM: About us it was growing darker, and I had to look hard to see
her face, which I meant always to carry with me; the closest, realest face at the
very bottom of memory.

> *He holds her hand.*

JIM: I'll come back. I promise.

ÁNTONIA: Maybe you will. But even if you don't, you're here.

SCENE 9: JIM AND ÁNTONIA: TWENTY YEARS ON

(NARRATOR JIM is onstage alone.)

NARRATOR JIM: Life intervened, and it was twenty years before I kept my promise. I married and became general counsel of one of the great western railways out of New York. I heard about Ántonia from time to time; that she married soon after I last saw her and she had had a hard life.

Perhaps it was cowardice that kept me away for so long. I kept putting it off until the next business trip. I didn't want to find her aged and broken. In the course of twenty crowded years one parts with many illusions. I didn't wish to lose the early ones.

I owe it to Lena Lingard that I finally made it. I was in San Francisco where both Tiny and Lena live. Both of them are single, self-reliant and wealthy women. Lena urged me to make the visit.

On my way east I broke my journey in Nebraska, arrived in Black Hawk, and set off to find her farm. At a little past mid-day, I arrived at my destination.

> *(Lights shift to a bright, golden yellow. The ensemble runs on with great energy and child-like enthusiasm to create the Cuzak farm. One huge, beautiful surprising element should be introduced, a large scrim decorated lavishly with great stalks of sunflowers, for example. The ensemble members begin chasing each other so that we sense children at play, but they are obscured. If you don't have a scrim, find some other way to communicate the presence of bucolic splendor alongside kinetic, youthful energy. JIM enters the scene. He is 40 now.)*

JIM *(calling out to the boys hidden among the foliage)*: Hello! Are you Mrs. Cuzak's children?

NINA: Yes!

JIM: Does she live up there on the hill?

LEO: Why do you want to know?!

JAN *(running off)*: Mama! Mama!

ANNA: Come up to the house, sir. Mother will see you up there.

> *General commotion, the children excited by a visitor. ÁNTONIA appears. She is battered, grizzled, and worn in appearance, but not diminished in character.*

ÁNTONIA: My husband's not home, sir. Can I do anything for you?

JIM: Don't you remember me, Tony?

> *Pause.*
> *Upon her realization, ÁNTONIA rushes to JIM to grab his hands or to hug him tightly.*

ÁNTONIA: Jim! Oh! JIM! Anna, Yulka, Jan, it's Jim Burden! *(Suddenly serious.)* What's happened? Is anybody dead?

JIM: What? No! I got off the train at Hastings and . . . drove to see you. I wanted to meet your family.

ÁNTONIA: Anna, Yulka, Jan, where are you all? Run, Anna, and hunt for the boys. And call Leo—where is that Leo?!? You don't have to go right off, do you, Jim? My oldest boy's not here. He's gone with Papa to the street fair in Wilber. Oh, who am I kidding—I won't let you go!

JIM: I have plenty of time. I was hoping to stay the night if that's alright.

ÁNTONIA: Yes! Children! Come meet Jim Burden, the one I've told you so much about!

The children run past. They eventually line up for her.

ÁNTONIA: I can't believe you're here. I bet you wouldn't have recognized me on the street, would you? But, no matter: I feel as young as I used to. We have plenty of help now.

JIM: You sure do!

ÁNTONIA: Tell me everything, how many kids have you got?

JIM: None.

ÁNTONIA: Oh. You're married, yes?

JIM: Mm-hm.

ÁNTONIA: Who is she?

JIM: Now, tell me the names of all your children.

ÁNTONIA: Oh, well, there's eleven of them now—

JIM: Eleven!

ÁNTONIA: I hope I can keep them straight! Two of them are with Papa at the street fair in Wilber. Wait until we show you the orchard! I've tended it like a baby. Number twelve!

NINA: And the fruit cellar, mama!

ÁNTONIA: Yes!

JAN: Mr. Burden, will you tell us about the rattler you find at the dog-town. How long was he for real?

LEO: Sometime mother say six feet and sometimes she say five. I say it was just a worm! Pbbbbtt!

JIM laughs.

ÁNTONIA: Oh, we have time and time for all the stories.

JIM: We have years and years!

> *Children cheer.*
> *The children and ÁNTONIA congregate around JIM.*

Scene 10: Farewell

NARRATOR JIM: I left Ántonia and her family early the next morning. I walked through Black Hawk , but most of my old friends were dead or had moved away. Strange children, who meant nothing to me, were playing in the Harlings' yard when I passed.

　　As I wandered over those rough pastures, I had the good luck to stumble upon a bit of the first road that went from Black Hawk out to my grandfather's farm. I thought about beginnings.

> *JIM and ÁNTONIA enter, run past NARRATOR JIM. They are young again.*
> *Eager and excited. The voices overlap.*

OTTO (*from offstage*): Burden! Looking for Jim Burden!

ÁNTONIA (*calling out*): Everybody! Come see what Jim kill! Come see! Hurry, Jim! So slow!

GRANDMOTHER (*voice-over*): Do you know who I am?

LENA (*voice-over*): You're going, but you haven't gone yet, have you?

JIM (*laughing*): Wait up!

> *They exit.*

NARRATOR JIM: This was the road over which Ántonia and I came on that night when we got off the train at Black Hawk, wondering children, being taken we knew not where. I had only to close my eyes to hear the rumbling of the wagons in the dark. The feelings of that night were so near that I could reach out and touch them with my hand. I had the sense of coming home to myself, and of having found out what a little circle man's experience is. For Ántonia and for me, this had been the road of Destiny. Now I understood that the same road was to bring us together again. Whatever we had missed, we possessed together the precious, the incommunicable past.

> *Train whistle.*
> *Blackout.*

Made in the USA
Lexington, KY
10 August 2014